C · L · A · S · I · C
SPORTS
Cars

C·L·A·S·S·I·C
SPORTS
Cars

the
apple
press

A QUINTET BOOK

Published by Apple Press Ltd.
293 Gray's Inn Road,
London WC1X 8QF

ISBN 1 85076 068 3

This book was designed and produced by
Quintet Publishing Limited
6 Blundell Street London N7

Art Director: Peter Bridgewater
Editors: Mark Chivers, Sarah Goodwin

Typeset in Great Britain by
Central Southern Typesetters, Eastbourne
Manufactured in Hong Kong by
Regent Publishing Services Limited
Printed in Hong Kong by
Leefung-Asco Printers Limited

The author and publishers would like to
thank the following for supplying
pictures:

Aston Martin Lagonda Ltd, pp.113–118;
J. Baker Collection, p.77; Chris Harvey,
pp.24–25, 26–27, 33, 38–63, 71, 90–91;
Long Island Automotive Museum,
pp.10–11, 14–15, 40–41, 49, 52–53;
Midland Motor Museum, pp.12–13, 16–
17; Mirco Decet, pp.68–69, 84–85, 86–87,
96, 97, 102, 108; Andrew Morland,
pp.28–29, 30–31, 34, 35, 38–39, 40–41,
46, 47, 48–49, 50–51, 53, 58–59, 64, 65,
66–67, 68, 69, 71, 72, 78–79, 80–81, 82,
83, 89, 92, 93, 94, 95; Performance Car
Magazine, pp.2, 15, 18, 19, 20–21, 22, 23,
36–37, 42–43, 44, 45, 59, 69, 78–79,
82–83, 98–99, 100–101, 106–107, 108–
109, 110–111, 114–115, 116–117, 118–
119, 121, 123, 124–125, 127.

Every effort has been made by the
publishers to trace the owners of the
photographs used in this book, and we
apologize for any inadvertent omissions.

Contents

INTRODUCTION

Almost as soon as the car was invented, there were those who saw it as something more than just a noisy new method of getting from one place to another.

Even before the turn of the century, when motoring in any form was an adventure in itself, racing had become well established. While cars for the road were still generally lightly built and of no great power, the specialized demands of long distance racing, over often appalling roads, had created a new breed of massively built, big-engined cars, built with competition as their sold aim? They were sporting cars, certainly, but they were not sportscars.

As motoring began to become a little more civilized in its basic, everyday roadgoing role, a mongrel mixture of road car and racing car began to appear – cars built to satisfy the whims of those who wanted something more than basic transport, but would settle for rather less than the perils of racing.

By the first decade of the twentieth century, early motoring enthusiasts were demanding more style, more individuality and, almost always, more performance – challenges which the early car designers and builders, pioneers themselves, were only too happy to rise to, and their patrons more than willing to pay for.

And so the sportscar was born.

It is virtually impossible to say definitively what was the first of the breed, or even where it originated.

Europe (predictably enough given its early motoring lead) has the most claimants. Prominent among them are the stripped Mercedes 60 h.p. tourers which successfully stood in for the 90 h.p. racing cars destroyed by fire before the 1903 Gordon Bennett Cup Race. In fact, the big Mercedes were just a one-off expediency that happened to work in an adapted role. A more convincing European claimant is the 1912 Hispano-Suiza Alfonso, a car small enough to be practical for everyday use, yet incorporating the very best of contemporary technology and a real sense of style.

Style was also something that marked out the early U.S. models, where the motor industry was rapidly gaining momentum. Generally considered the earliest American sportscar is the Apperson Jack Rabbit of 1904. This was another multi-purpose vehicle, built in Indiana – appropriately enough by great-great-grandsons of the pioneer Daniel Boone. While the Apperson remained relatively unknown, cars like the later Stutz Bearcat and Mercer Raceabout, almost caricatures of the current American racing car style, are the ones remembered today as the earliest American sportscar image.

Now that motoring is into its second century, it is still apparently impossible for enthusiasts to agree on an exact definition of what makes a sportscar.

The definition, admittedly, has itself changed over the years. In particular, it has changed in the way the sportscar has become ever more remote from the racing car, as racing has become more specialized and more technology-dominated; it has changed with the car itself, from being *only* expensively exclusive to

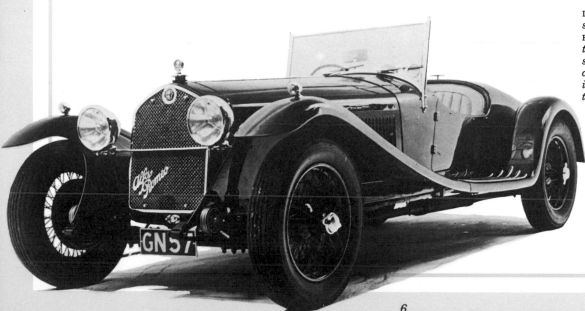

LEFT *Graceful Alfa-Romeo two-seater of the 1930s.*
RIGHT *1932 poster advertising the Bugatti in typical Art Deco style. Bugatti had just abandoned single-cam engines in favour of the state-of-the-art twin overhead cam.*

being both expensively exclusive *and* cheaply popular; and, not least, it has changed to keep pace with legislation – never more evidently than post 1960, when the open top, formerly a prerequisite of the sportscar – all but disappeared, to make a brief comeback as the symbol of the freedom which the sportscar embodies.

Most of all, the idea of a sportscar has rarely had universal currency: somehow, an MG or a Bentley could only be English, a Mercedes or a BMW is all Teutonic efficiency, the Alfa Romeos or Ferraris or Lamborghinis of this world all Italian brio – and a Corvette, any Corvette, could *only* be American. The very few cars that have made the transition between Europe and America are classic exceptions which prove the rules.

Whatever the prevailing definition, there are very few motoring enthusiasts who could not recognize a sportscar, from whatever era, or whatever country of origin, when they saw it.

As for physical characteristics, there are those who would immediately cite 'wind-in-the-hair', and it is difficult to deny the appeal of the soft-top, but that alone certainly doesn't make a car a sportscar. Many of the really great sportscars, in fact most of the comparatively recent ones, are tin-topped, while just taking the top off a saloon, whatever its other attributes, doesn't necessarily turn it into a sportscar.

Nor does giving the same saloon 150mph performance make it a sportscar; many sportscars *do* have exceptional top speeds, or staggering acceleration, or both – but quite a few *great* sportscars have neither. The archetypal popular sportscar of the 1940s, for instance, the T-series MGs, could barely beat 70mph. This was at a time when several saloon cars were already capable of much more speed, but the little MG, one of the first sportscars to be totally accepted on *both* sides of the Atlantic, is every bit as much of a classic as the Ferrari Daytona of the late 1960s, which could out-run it by a comfortable 100mph.

Performance is only a part of it. Perhaps more important than outright speed and acceleration is some special combination of roadholding and handling which enables the sportscar, be it ever so humble, to use whatever power it has to the full, anywhere and any time. All the great sportscars have that common characteristic – yet, again, it is not one that is exclusive to what we choose to call a sportscar; quite a number of saloons and tourers which have immaculate road manners still don't fill the sportscar bill.

Looks are another guide, but not a totally reliable one. There have always been cars whose looks promised more sporting prowess than they delivered, and just having a Bentley, Bugatti or a Mercedes badge doesn't automatically turn a sporty tourer into a sportscar. Since the advent of replicas, some of which are excellent but most of which aren't, that is even more true; underneath many a latter day Bugatti lurks the heart of a Beetle . . .

Perhaps the sportscar is really more an attitude of mind than anything else. What it is really about is plain and simple fun. All the cars in the following pages offer that; some combine it with sophistication, some sacrifice the frills for cheap availability, but who is to say that the owner of a 1930s SS100 or a 1950s Triumph had any less fun than today's Lamborghini or Porsche pilot?

In the final analysis, the sportscar today is exactly the same as it always has been right through its history: a scream of individuality and a clamour of something more than the mean – for both the builder and the buyer. It has survived everything that politics, economics and legislation have ever thrown at it and cars like the mass-market Toyota MR2 or the stunning MG EX-E prototype show that manufacturers big and small, east and west, still see the sportscar as part of our motoring future.

So long as motoring enthusiasts exist, the sportscar will exist for them.

LEFT *This illustration from an early Hispano-Suiza catalogue shows one of the world's first sports cars, the Alphonse XIII, named for King Alfonso of Spain, an early motoring enthusiast.*
RIGHT *Watercolour painting by Gaston Maurié of the winning De Dietrich car in the French Eliminating Races held at Clermont-Ferrand in 1905.*

1911 MERCER 35R RACEABOUT

Before the Mercer Automobile Co in Mercer County, N.J., introduced the Mercer Type 35 Raceabout in 1911, there were racing cars and there were sporting versions of touring cars. The racing cars typically comprised very big engines shoehorned into massive chassis, stripped to the bare bones and with minimal bodywork – all in an effort to save weight. In their rudimentary way, they were as specialised as any racing car of today and definitely not for everyday use. The sporting cars were generally little more than touring cars divested of the heavier creature comforts to improve performance.

The new Mercer though was something else. It was perhaps the first car that could genuinely be called a 'sportscar'; it was neither a single-purpose racing car nor a compromised tourer, but a car designed specifically for everyday motoring excitement, with more than just a dash of style.

That may not be a complete definition of a sportscar, but any car which fulfils it is well on its way to qualifying for the name.

The Raceabout was designed by Mercer's new chief engineer, Finley Robertson Porter, as a road car which could also be used as a racer by the amateur sportsman – and there was no shortage of those in pre-World War I America. It had a four-cylinder 55 h.p. T-head engine, two bucket seats, a handbrake, gearshift – four wheels and not much else. Even the throttle pedal was outboard of the driver's seat.

As an option, the Mercer driver could order a distinctive monocle windshield that fitted onto the long, exposed steering column – the sum total of weather protection for the Raceabout driver and his passenger!

The bodywork involved no more than a low bonnet, long rakish wings (with small running boards), and a massive bolster fuel tank on the tail, surmounted by two spare tyres on detachable rims. Mercer tended to go the whole hog and paint the already rather conspicuous Raceabout in garish colours with flamboyant pinstriping. One of the most popular schemes was a bright sunshine yellow with black.

It was definitely a car to be seen in, but it was more than just a pretty face; it also backed up its looks with performance. Mercer guaranteed the standard Raceabout to have a top speed of at least 70mph/113kph which was certainly enough to leave most other cars of the day trailing by a handsome margin, and with

its very light weight it would reach such speeds in spirited fashion.

The penalty of the light weight, shortish wheelbase and hard, semi-elliptic springing was a spectacularly lively ride on the often appalling roads of the day. However, the steering was light and precise, the gearshift incredibly slick by prevailing standards, and the roadholding was a tail-sliding delight. The brakes were terrible, but that never seemed to stop

the Mercer driver from using his car's performance to the full.

The Raceabout was not just an expensive toy either; at a very reasonable $2,250 in 1911 it created a large market for itself and the imitators which inevitably followed. Best known among these was the Stutz Bearcat, which had most of the Raceabout's looks but far from all its performance.

The racing versions of the Raceabout were used to great effect by such all-American heroes as Barney Oldfield and Ralph de Palma. In 1913 Spencer Wishart took a racing type 35F, the smallest car in

the race, to second place at Indianapolis and in 1914 Eddie Pullen won the American Grand Prize for Mercer, who now advertised the Raceabout as 'The Champion Light Car'.

Unfortunately, as well as being perhaps the first real sportscar, the Raceabout was also one of the first to demonstrate that manufacturers can easily ignore the potential of their models. When Porter left in 1914, Mercer went on to replace the classic 35R with a stodgy, L-head engined model, the 22/70 Raceabout, which, tellingly, was also available as a touring model.

1911 MERCER 35R RACEABOUT	
Engine	Continental in-line, 4-cyl, T-head
Capacity	4.9 litres
Maximum power	55bhp
Chassis/suspension	Ladder chassis, semi-elliptic all round
Top speed	70mph+
0–60mph	—

BELOW *Lightweight (and almost non-existent!) bodywork coupled with a 4.9 litre engine, gave the Mercer Raceabout sparkling acceleration and a 70 mph/112 kph+ top-speed. Creature comforts are few and far between, and stopping the car is a bit of a problem, but who cares? Available in only the most garish colours, the Raceabout is definitely the car to be seen in!*

1912 HISPANO-SUIZA ALFONSO

If the American Mercer Raceabout could stake a claim to being the first sportscar in the world, the Hispano-Suiza Alfonso, introduced shortly after the Mercer in 1911, had an equally strong claim as the first production sportscar in Europe.

It was designed by the great Swiss engineer Marc Birkigt, Hispano-Suiza's young technical director, and based on his successful voiturette racing design of 1909. A long-stroke 2.6-litre development of that car won the Coupe de l'Auto GP des Voiturettes in 1910 and this first of several Hispanos to bear the Alfonso name emerged the following year, as a production version of the voiturette, with a side-valve four-cylinder engine, further enlarged to 3.6 litres.

It became available in a number of two- and four-seater versions; all of them with the same sporting character, and they took their name from Hispano's enthusiastic royal patron, King Alfonso XIII – of Spain, where the Hispano-Suiza company had been founded in 1904.

It was one of the few Spanish-built Hispanos to achieve any special distinction. All the great Hispanos of later years, mostly much larger and more complex cars than the Alfonso, came from the French branch of the company, set up in 1911, initially as an assembly plant for the Spanish cars, but later as a manufacturer in its own right. Although the Spanish factory in Barcelona made far more cars than the French operation, they were mostly just cheaper versions of the French models.

French built versions of the extremely popular Alfonso soon went into production and for a while there were even plans to build the model in Russia, a possibility which was eventually frustrated by the outbreak of World War I.

By the heavyweight standards of the day, the Alfonso looked almost frail, with a high chassis (available in either short- or long-wheelbase versions), delicate looking wings and narrow, wire-spoked wheels. Its looks, however, belied a rugged design typical of Birkigt's original thinking.

The 3.6-litre engine was notable mainly for its very long stroke – more than twice the bore size and a feature originally prompted by racing rules. It gave about 65bhp at something less than 2,500rpm, which was enough to give the compact little car a top speed in the region of 75mph/121kph – plus exceptional

1912 HISPANO-SUIZA 'ALFONSO'	
Engine	In-line, 4-cyl, SV
Capacity	3.6 litres
Maximum power	65bhp
Chassis/suspension	Ladder chassis, semi-elliptic all round
Top speed	75mph
0–60mph	—

ABOVE AND RIGHT *Delicate-looking bodywork disguises a rugged chassis design. Its lightness gives the car good handling, and underneath lies a powerful racing-derived, 3.6-litre engine.*

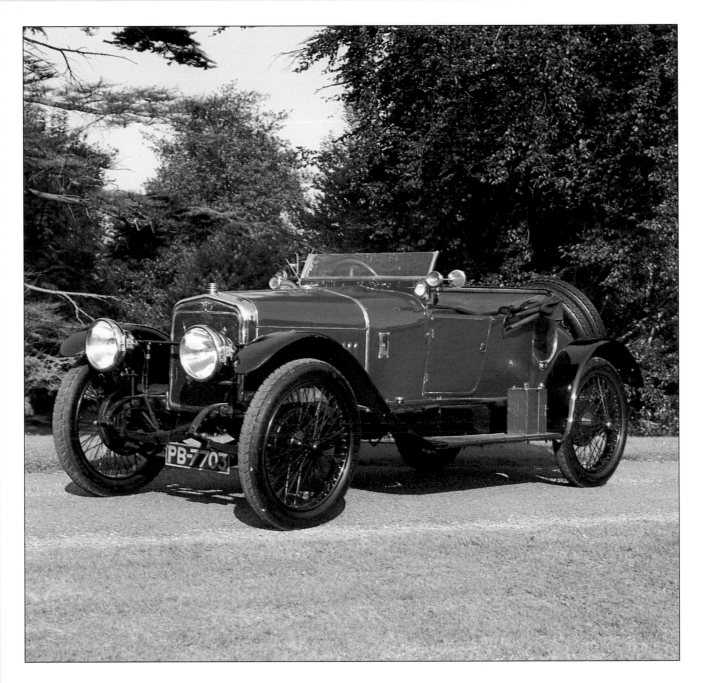

flexibility thanks to the torque typical of the long stroke layout. This engine was installed in unit with the gearbox, unlike most of its contemporaries which still tended to treat the latter as a separate component, often accommodated somewhere quite remote from the engine.

Even in 1911, there were faster cars than the Alfonso, but only either out-and-out racing cars or a very few large tourers. Where the Alfonso really differed was in its nimbleness and, like the Mercer Raceabout, in its style. The Mercer had been able to run rings round the generally much more powerful opposition in its racing days and those similar handling characteristics were successfully transferred to the Alfonso – but without demanding the

skills of a racing driver to make use of them.

For once, it was not the manufacturer who was responsible for the demise of a classic model but in this case the onset of World War I. Although the Spanish factory continued to build cars more or less throughout the war, it obviously considered the Alfonso to be somewhat inappropriate for the climate of the period and concentrated instead on larger touring cars.

The French factories built large numbers of Birkigt-designed aero-engines and after hostilities had ceased put their wartime profits and engineering lessons to good use with some magnificent luxury cars – but never again anything quite so sporty as the Alfonso.

1928 BUGATTI TYPE 43

When people talk of genius in the same breath as the motor car, they will usually talk of one man: Ettore Bugatti. Genius may be the right sentiment but the wrong word; Bugatti was really an artist whose medium happened to be motor cars – and like most artists he combined eccentricity with his brilliance.

Bugatti, born in Milan in 1881, came from a family of artists. His father was an architect and furniture-maker whose work is now highly regarded. His younger brother was a distinguished sculptor, but although Ettore dabbled in the fine arts he was always more drawn to mechanical designs.

He had no formal engineering training; he designed essentially by eye, with a seemingly intuitive appreciation of material strength which he steadfastly declined to back with conventional calculations.

His other great passion was for thoroughbred horses and he obviously saw parallels in designing thoroughbred cars; he even referred to his line of cars as 'le pur-sang' – literally, thoroughbred.

He designed his first car in 1901, before working on designs for several manufacturers, one of which subsequently re-emerged in 1909 as the prototype Bugatti, in production from 1910.

Almost from the beginning he entered his cars in races and adapted the lessons of the racetrack to his sporting road cars. His greatest racing success was as much commercial as sporting; the legendary Type 35 Grand Prix car and its derivatives were designed not just as cars for the works team but also as 'over the counter' racers. Not only did they become probably the most successful racing cars of all time, they also contributed greatly to one of Bugatti's finest road cars – the Type 43.

The Type 43, introduced in 1927, used a very slightly detuned version of the Type 35B Grand Prix car's supercharged 2.3-litre straight-eight engine in a chassis derived from the underpowered Type 38 tourer, the main difference being a slightly shorter wheelbase. What this created was the world's first 100mph production car, not just in the fanciful realms of a catalogue or on a closed race track, but for real, on almost any decent road. In fact the 43 was good for at least 110mph, or supposedly as much as 125mph with the optional higher final drive ratio – at

RIGHT A true supercar in its day, and no slouch even by today's standards, the Bugatti Type 43 is quite literally a racing car for the road. The first production car to be capable of more than 100 mph/160 kph, its supercharged eight-cylinder engine would whisk it to a 110 mph/176 kph maximum in fourth gear alone!

BELOW *Classic lines of the Type 43 conceal the secret of Bugatti's success. The chassis, suspension and brakes are all superbly engineered to give the car handling and stopping power to match its performance.*

1928 BUGATTI TYPE 43	
Engine	In-line, 8-cyl, sohc
Capacity	2.3 litres
Maximum power	120bhp
Chassis/suspension	Ladder chassis, semi-elliptic front, quarter-elliptic rear
Top speed	110mph
0–60mph	11.7 seconds

a time when 70mph was considered quick for a production car.

It was sold, very expensively, as a 3½-seater sports tourer, the odd half being an occasional seat alongside a full-sized rear seat. The engineering was typically Bugatti; the engine, externally square-cut and plain looking, concealed its artistry inside. It also concealed one of Bugatti's weaknesses, a built-up crankshaft with roller bearings and no forced lubrication, which he stubbornly ignored even though it was plainly necessary. This crank was lovely to look at but like much of Bugatti's work needed constant attention to his own standards to keep it serviceable.

When all was well its 120bhp and massive torque gave the 43 quite remarkable performance. It was flexible enough to take the car from a standstill to maximum speed in top gear. More conventionally, through the slick, four-speed gearbox, with the supercharger taking effect above about 1500rpm, it would reach 60mph in less than 12 seconds and cover a standing quarter-mile in only 17 seconds.

This performance was matched by a superb chassis – the secret of much of Bugatti's success, but again dependant on the car being maintained to Bugatti standards. Very firm suspension, semi-elliptic at the front and quarter-elliptic at the back, with friction shock absorbers, was hung on an elegant, rigid chassis and gave precise, grippy handling with feedback worthy of any racing car. Its brakes were probably the best of its day, cable operated but brilliantly laid out to give positive servo action through their own torque reaction – the brighter side of Bugatti's genius.

The Bugatti remains the archetype of the supremely elegant sports car, the epitome of an Art Deco car. It is also notorious as the car that caused the death of the American dancer Isadora Duncan, who was strangled when her fashionably long scarf became entangled in the wire wheels as she speeded along.

The 43 was made until 1931, latterly as an over-bodied American-inspired version, the 43A. In a way it contributed to its own demise. Bugatti gave three 43s to American racing star Leon Duray in exchange for two track racing Miller cars in which Duray had campaigned in Europe. Bugatti based his own first twin-cam engine design, the Type 51 racer, on the fabulous Millers – and its roadgoing derivative, the 55, ultimately replaced the 43.

1930 4½-LITRE 'BLOWER' BENTLEY

If there is any single universal image of the vintage sportscar, the 'Blower' Bentley is undoubtedly it. The massive British Racing Green cars which Bentley's arch-rival Ettore Bugatti is alleged to have described as 'les plus vites camions du monde' – the fastest trucks in the world – are the cars that most people think of as the Bentleys that won Le Mans; in that at least they are mistaken.

The racing 'Blower' cars, strictly speaking, were not even built by Bentley themselves; W. O. Bentley personally hated them and all they stood for. What the company did build was the run of 50 or so super-charged 4½-litre production cars which regulations demanded be offered for sale in order to qualify the model for international racing. W.O. did so under protest, grudgingly allocating a corner of his Crickle-wood factory to producing touring and sportscars with the blown engine.

Specifically, his objection was to supercharging, which he held to be a vastly inferior and less reliable route to more power than increasing capacity. He was more or less forced into accepting the blower idea by the financial state of his company, which at the time was existing largely through the backing of the enor-mously wealthy Woolf Barnato.

Both Barnato and Bentley saw racing as important to the company. Barnato as a driver (as well as the company chairman) and Bentley as a salesman; they simply didn't agree on methods.

While the production cars were built in the works, however reluctantly, the racing cars were built by the ostensibly private Birkin-Paget racing team in Welwyn Garden City (now a London suburb). Birkin was the racing driver Sir Henry 'Tim' Birkin, and Paget was the Hon. Dorothy Paget, the team's bene-factress.

There were only four of the real, racing 'Blower' Bentleys, each of them different and none of them, in spite of popular misconceptions, particularly success-ful. The first became a single seater, the second a short-wheelbase four-seater, the third a longer four-seater and the last, completed in 1930 (and the most successful of the four), a short-chassis car which, stripped to the bare necessities, finished second in the 1930 Pau Grand Prix, driven by Birkin himself.

The unsupercharged 'works' 4½-litre Bentley (whose development from the earlier 3-litre four-

cylinder model had been paid for by Barnato) had won Le Mans in 1928 (Barnato himself sharing the driving with Bernard Rubin), but the blown cars were not even ready to put up a fight in the 1929 running of the 24-Hour classic. Instead, W.O. was able to gloat over yet another works victory gained by an unsupercharged car – in this case the 6½-litre Speed Six, which had been his answer to the 'Blower'

as a way to increasing performance.

Whatever W.O.'s personal misgivings, the big supercharged car is indisputably a classic. The production cars, of which the 26 open Vanden Plas-bodied cars at least looked like the racers, could boast about 175bhp, but the Birkin cars could muster over 250bhp at a very low 3750rpm. That, combined with staggering torque at almost any engine speed, was enough to give even this two-ton-plus car exceptional performance.

On the long Mulsanne straight at Le Mans (after which the turbocharged 1980s Bentley is named) the big Blower 4½ might have touched around 130mph. It took maybe 8½ seconds to get to 50mph but after that its massive power gave it enormous high speed flexibility, which was just as well, as the gearbox, though extremely strong, was extraordinarily awkward to use.

The roadholding was surprisingly good, and the handling was certainly very forgiving, but there was no disguising how much kinetic energy the huge drum brakes had to destroy from very high speeds.

It all matters very little, of course; no-one is particularly interested in the shortcomings of a car like the big Bentley; to the man in the street it is still one of the greatest of all classic sportscars.

1930 BENTLEY 4½-LITRE S/C	
Engine	In-line, 4-cyl, sohc, s/c, 16v
Capacity	4.5 litres
Maximum power	250bhp
Chassis/suspension	Ladder chassis, semi-elliptic all round
Top speed	130mph
0–60mph	8.5 seconds

LEFT AND OVERLEAF *The classic supercharged 4½-litre Bentley.*

ABOVE *British engineering at its best – the cockpit of the 'Blower' Bentley.*

UR 6571

1932 ALFA ROMEO 8C MONZA

The Alfa Romeo 8C is a car for all reasons. In various guises, it was a Le Mans winner (four times in a row), a Grand Prix winner (on circuits as diverse as the super-fast Monza autodrome and the tight, round-the-houses Monte Carlo street circuit), and it was also a superb roadgoing sportscar.

Even by today's standards it is exceptionally quick, particularly in its classic Monza 2,600 guise, but it is also a car which can quite easily serve for everyday use – a sportscar by any definition.

The 8C series was Alfa's sporting mainstay from its introduction in sports racing form in 1931 right through to the enforced end of production in 1939 with the onset of World War II. It was designed by the greatest of all Alfa Romeo's engineers, Vittorio Jano, who had joined the company in September, 1923. He was enticed over to Alfa from Fiat's racing department by Enzo Ferrari – who became famous as a racing driver and team organiser with Alfa Romeo long before he began to build cars under his own name. Fiat were not very pleased with Jano's defection, but Alfa Romeo were delighted . . .

The 8C first appeared in long wheelbase 2,300 sportscar format, early in 1931. On its radiator cowl was the distinctive Alfa Romeo badge, combining the red-on-white St George's Cross of Alfa's native Milan and the bizarre emblem of the ancient Milanese rulers, the Viscontis – a writhing, crowned serpent swallowing a small child. The laurel wreath which surrounds the badge commemorates Alfa Romeo's victory in the first official world championship, achieved in 1924 with Jano's very first Alfa design, the all-conquering P2 Grand Prix car.

In May, 1931, only weeks after its introduction, the sports version of the 8C won the gruelling Targa Florio road race in Sicily. Two weeks later two short-

LEFT AND ABOVE RIGHT *Like many cars of the period, the Alfa Romeo Monza is super-charged to give it truly remarkable acceleration and a top speed of 135 mph/216 kph. The comfortable, well-laid-out cockpit is relatively roomy, and has surprisingly comprehensive instrumentation.*

chassis models, stripped of lights, wings and other non-essential running gear, were entered in the Italian Grand Prix at Monza. They finished first and second and the rare short-chassis racing model has been known as the Monza ever since.

The heart of the 8C is Jano's magnificent, supercharged, twin-overhead-cam, straight-eight engine. It started life as a 2.3-litre unit but later grew to 2.6-litres, originally in the racing team cars run by Ferrari and, later, through modification, in many customer cars. It is a beautiful looking-engine, with its long twin cam-covers and its heavily finned inlet manifolding leading from the Roots-type supercharger, which, like the camshafts, is driven from a central vertical gear-train between the individual halves of the all-alloy engine.

It is a very strong unit, superbly balanced and quite capable of much higher revs than most of its contemporaries. Even in its sports versions it was good for somewhere near 150bhp and the works racing Monzas gave as much as 180bhp, while remaining perfectly tractable and trouble-free.

Although the Monza was quite definitely a racing model, it also makes a very impressive roadgoing sportscar. Its cockpit is roomier and more comfortable than might be expected from its vintage, and its controls are surprisingly modern in layout – the only exception being the placing of the throttle pedal

between clutch and brakes, a layout common to many cars of its period.

From behind the big steering wheel it actually feels quite small and its performance is truly remarkable. A Monza geared for short sprints will reach 60mph/96.5kph in less than seven seconds and at the other end of the scale might approach 140mph/225kph.

On rock-hard suspension and damping its ride is bumpy but its smooth surface grip is astonishing. Its quick, accurate steering and powerful, mechanically operated brakes make it a delightful car to drive even in the 1980s, especially as today's improved road surfaces give a smoother ride than would have been possible in the 1930s.

What it must have felt like in its day is surely the true measure of Jano's genius.

1932 ALFA ROMEO 8C MONZA	
Engine	In-line, 8-cyl, 2ohc, s/c
Capacity	2.6 litres
Maximum power	150bhp (180bhp for racing)
Chassis/suspension	Ladder chassis, semi-elliptic all round
Top speed	135mph
0–60mph	7.0 seconds

1935 AUBURN 851 SPEEDSTER

If imitation is the sincerest form of flattery, there can be little doubt that Auburn's various Speedsters have been flattered from the day they were made. The spectacularly sporty-looking cars became style leaders in the age of style, and right up to the present day they have inspired numerous replica builders both in America and Europe.

Anyone who dismisses replicas as nothing more than a mish-mash of other people's bits and pieces would do well to look at the original Speedsters. Like most Auburns, they were assembled around unsophisticated 'proprietary' engines, and running gear from the company parts bin. What made the Speedsters memorable where the vast majority of Auburns were eminently forgettable was their combination of brash styling and promise of near racing car performance, at least in Auburn's skilful sales pitches. They owed more, in fact, to one man's incredible talent as a salesman than to any particular engineering excellence.

The man was Errett Lobban Cord, who eventually linked the name of Auburn with those of Cord and Duesenberg in a classic trilogy of American sporting marques, but who arrived at Auburn, in 1924, at a time when the company was close to bankruptcy on the strength of an image of extreme mediocrity. Cord, who by his mid-20s had already made and lost several fortunes, revamped Auburn's dowdy range, treated them to a major sales splash and turned the name into a respectable seller.

As ever, competition exposure played its part, as Auburn began to take part in stock car racing and record breaking – and the sporting image was cleverly exploited in pulling customers who had no real intention of buying a sportscar into the corporate showrooms.

The first Speedster, sensationally styled by Count Alexis de Sakhnoffsky, appeared in 1928 on the eight-cylinder, Lycoming-engined 8-115 chassis, establishing its performance credentials with a 108mph run at Daytona Beach. Even more surprising than the Speedster's performance though was its price, which was less than half that of its most obvious rival, the Stutz Black Hawk. Not surprisingly, it helped Auburn to its best sales year to date.

Cord made one of his occasional mistakes in 1929, with the spectacular Cabin Speedster sedan; long,

ABOVE *Flamboyant styling makes the Auburn Speedster really stand out from the crowd, while the supercharged, straight-eight engine makes sure it goes as well as it looks. Every car guaranteed to top 100 mph/160 kph!*

low, racily streamlined and with every possible weight-saving trick, including wicker seats, it was just a bit too much of a good thing and though most people marvelled, very few bought. Cord quickly reverted to slightly more conservative models and gave Auburn its best ever sales year in the middle of the 1930s depression, topping off his audacious marketing style in 1932 by offering the first and last twelve-cylinder car ever to be sold for less than $1000 – with the inevitable Speedster option at only $1600.

Whether it was the depression or the thought that a V12, even a Lycoming-engined V12, was too good to be true at the price, the car didn't sell and it was dropped in 1934, to make way in 1935 for the greatest of all the Speedsters, the classic Type 851.

The 851, styled almost as a parody of the earlier models by Gordon Buehrig, had the archetypal pointed tail, a huge bonnet (hood) (which in this case housed a centrifugally supercharged straight-eight Lycoming engine of about 150bhp), vast, flexible outside exhaust pipes and a short two-seater cabin behind a tiny, steeply-raked windscreen. On the dashboard of every 851 was a small plaque which guaranteed that the car had exceeded 100mph on test

in the hands of Auburn racer and and record breaker Ab Jenkins.

It was indeed a staggering performer, with an easily selected option of high or low axle ratios for top speed or acceleration, but every 851 was sold at a loss. A very slightly revised model, the 852, replaced the 851 in 1936 but time was running out for Auburn and the 500 or so 851/852 Speedsters sold became Auburn's monument rather than its saviour as the company went out of business in 1937. Here is another example of a superb car that is no longer in production due to management problems, despite the excellence of the product.

1935 AUBURN SPEEDSTER	
Engine	Lycoming in-line, 8-cyl, sv, s/c
Capacity	4.6 litres
Maximum power	150bhp
Chassis/suspension	Ladder chassis, semi-elliptic all round
Top speed	100mph+
0–60mph	—

1935 SS100 JAGUAR

Although Jaguar did not appear as a make in its own right until 1945, its history goes back well beyond that. It began in the British seaside resort of Blackpool with the Swallow Sidecar Co, which built motorcycle sidecars in the early 1920s, then grew as the Swallow Sidecar and Coachbuilding Co, which built special, usually very sporty bodies on various makes of saloon car during the late 1920s.

From 1931 the company (which became known as SS Cars Ltd in 1933) built complete cars, though still initially using bought-in engines and chassis. The first of these were known as the SSI and SSII saloons, sporty cars, but not yet sportscars.

The company's first *real* sportscar appeared in March 1935: a rakish two-seater with a 2.7-litre, 86bhp, six-cylinder Standard side-valve engine in a shortened SSI underslung chassis. It was dubbed the SS90, alluding, slightly optimistically, to its top speed.

The company never actually admitted to what SS meant in their own minds: Super Sports, Super Swallow , Swallow Sports – take your pick.

Only 23 SS90s were built, up to September 1935 – when SS announced two new cars with overhead-valve engines. They were the SS Jaguar saloon and the SS Jaguar 100 – the logical development of the SS90.

What started as a model name quickly gained prominence, and in 1945, when SS wasn't exactly an ideal title, the company became Jaguar Cars Ltd.

The SS100, with its sweeping wings, wire wheels and huge, mesh-covered headlamps, looked very like the two-seater SS90 but was much better developed.

It used a purpose-built chassis rather than a cut-down saloon type, with an alloy body over an ash frame. It had a four-speed gearbox and non-indepen-

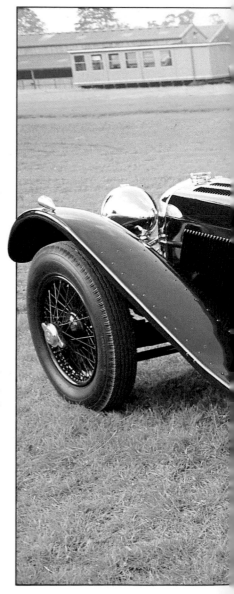

RIGHT *Performance and style at a budget price? The classic SS100 Jaguar sports car is a far cry from the company's original products – motorcycle sidecars. Faultless handling, superb brakes, and a willing, flexible engine make the SS100 a real driver's car.*

1935 SS100 3½-LITRE	
Engine	In-line, 6-cyl, ohv
Capacity	3.5 litres
Maximum power	125bhp
Chassis/suspension	Ladder chassis, semi-elliptic all round
Top speed	101mph
0–60mph	11.5 seconds

dent suspension all round, on long, semi-elliptic springs with a mixture of hydraulic and friction damping – basically like the SS90 but with improved mouldings. The big, finned drum brakes changed from cable to rod operation, but the biggest improvement of all was the new engine.

The overhead valve conversion and twin carbs put the quoted power output up to 100bhp and the 100 again represented the claimed top speed. As with the SS90, it was a bit optimistic to start with, by 4 or 5mph according to most tests, but the SS100, like Jaguars ever since, offered quite exceptional value for money – at only around one third of the price of a contemporary 'thoroughbred' of similar performance.

The 2.7-litre SS100 stayed in production until 1939 and a total of 198 were eventually built, but towards the end of 1937 the car was finally able to live up to its name when a 3.5-litre version was introduced alongside the 2.7.

The bigger engine, with slightly higher compression, offered 125bhp, great flexibility and a genuine roadgoing top speed of 101mph. Sparkling acceleration took it to 60mph in about 11½ seconds and to a standing quarter-mile in just 17 seconds.

Its roadholding and handling, with very quick steering, were impeccable – even if the ride was a bit hard – and its brakes were superb.

Just 116 3.5-litre SS100s were built before they too ceased production, in 1939. Of the total of 314 SS100s of both types which were built, probably 200 survive, most of them in the USA, where the Jaguar reputation for performance with style and value is now perhaps stronger than ever, one of the few British cars to enjoy such a reputation.

1937 BMW 328

Considering the strength of BMW's high-tech sporting image today, it is difficult to believe that the company's first venture as a car manufacturer was in building a version of the humble Austin Seven. BMW was already well known for its motorcycles and aeroengines (the famous quartered blue and white badge is the stylised blur of a spinning propellor) before it acquired the German manufacturing rights for the Seven, by taking over Dixi in 1928 and relaunching Dixi's interpretation of the Seven as the BMW 3/15, on New Year's Day 1929.

A close look at the way the 3/15 evolved showed that later developments were hardly surprising. It took BMW very little time to discover, as many had before them, that motor sporting success was a surefire way of selling motor cars and the German Seven soon became a very sporty car indeed. BMW offered the little car as either a roadster or open tourer and it started its four-wheel racing career by winning a

team prize in the 1929 Alpine Trial, followed by a class win in the 1930 Monte Carlo Rally.

The company's real sporting fame, however, sprang from the arrival in 1933 of its first six-cylinder model, the 303 saloon – a tiny car for a six, with just 1175cc and about 30bhp to its name! Predictably, this soon grew a little bit bigger and quicker as it evolved into the 1.5-litre 315, with twin

1937 BMW 328	
Engine	In-line, 6-cyl, sohc
Capacity	1.9 litres
Maximum power	80bhp
Chassis/suspension	Tubular, transverse leaf/wishbone ifs, semi-elliptic rear
Top speed	95mph
0–60mph	—

BELOW *Elegance and superb engineering rolled into one, sum up the BMW 328. Its advanced, wind-cheating bodywork looks good, while independent front suspension gives the 328 the comfort of a saloon car ride with racing car levels of roadholding.*

carburettors and a four-speed gearbox for 1934, but still only 34bhp.

Alongside the basic 315 however, BMW gave another hint of its true colours with the sporty 315/1 roadster, which had triple carbs, 40bhp and a top speed of over 75mph/121kph. This model was good enough to win the Alpine Trial outright among its many sporting successes, before it gave way to the next of the series, a little bit larger again, at 1.9-litres, the excellent 319.

The 319 was the final forerunner of the classic 328, which had none of the reticence of the previous models about its true character; it was a real sportscar through and through. It was unveiled in the summer of 1936 when it won the prestigious Eiffel-rennen sportscar race and it went on sale early in 1937. It was based on the 319's well-proven tubular chassis, now with an engine of close to 2 litres and using a clever hemispherical head design with inclined valves operated by a single camshaft and a crossover pushrod arrangement. This gave the new engine most of the advantages of a real twin-cam design but without the complexity and manufacturing expense.

The engine quickly earned a reputation for being both reliable and delightfully crisp. It also had a much increased power output; with three down-draught carbs (and the ability to use an unusually high compression ratio thanks to the advanced head design) it produced 80bhp and gave the roadgoing 328 a very respectable top speed of almost 95mph/153kph.

Additionally, it set new standards of roadholding and handling – with much of the refinement of a saloon car ride combined with racing car standards of grip. Much of that was due to the 328's brave insistence on using independent front suspension at a time when beam axles were generally the order of the day on sportscars, but it said even more about the overall integrity of the chassis design.

To complete this magnificent mechanical package, the BMW engineers came up with a beautiful and aerodynamically efficient body which made most other sportscars of the day look positively primitive. It even had a smooth full-length undertray to dramatically cut drag below the car.

Not only BMW themselves reaped the benefits of the 328; it was imported into Britain as the Frazer-Nash BMW and through that connection, as war reparations after World War II, it was adopted by Bristol as the basis of their new luxury sporting saloons. It was also widely used in racing for many years, even after the war.

BMW themselves may have lost out in the short term, but the engineering skills which created the 328 would not lay dormant for long.

1946 MG TC

Few cars come closer to the popular concept of a sportscar than the splendid MG TC Midget, introduced in November 1945 and in production until the end of 1949.

No car could have been a better celebration of the recent end of World War II. For not much more than the cost of a small saloon car, it brought cheap and cheerful wind-in-the-hair sporting motoring to thousands who could never have afforded it before – and might anyway never have had the freedom of spirit to drive such a car.

The TC was the archetypal British sportscar of the period, but more than that, it became known everywhere as the MG that took the British sportscar to America – although only just over 2000 were actually sold there, mostly around the sunny and always sportscar conscious west coast, from a total production run of exactly 10,000.

With lean, rakish lines derived from the small prewar MG sportscars, a simple steel ladder chassis and a long-stroke, overhead-valve 1250cc four-cylinder engine with twin carburettors, this third in the series of T-type Midgets was low on technology but very high on entertainment.

It was strictly a two-seater, in the pre-war style, with very little by way of luggage space but a surprisingly roomy and comfortable cockpit considering its compact exterior dimensions. Its lovely body had deeply cutaway doors, an impressively long, louvred bonnet (hood), a huge slab fuel tank, knock-on wire wheels and beautiful sweeping wings (fenders). It looked every inch the breath of freedom that the new postwar motoring market wanted, and it was.

It wasn't particularly fast, even by the generally mediocre standards of the time, and its mere 54bhp gave it a top speed of about 75mph – with 0–60mph taking a leisurely 22 seconds, or about twice as long as a very ordinary family saloon of today. But what it lacked in outright performance it more than made up for with its outstanding character and drivability.

It was so small and nimble that on the relatively uncluttered roads of the day it was possible to maintain near 60mph averages without ever needing to go over 70mph! The steering, with a massive sprung-spoke steering wheel on a telescopically adjustable column, was very quick (with less than two turns from lock-to-lock) and precise and the four gear ratios

1946 MG TC	
Engine	In-line, 4-cyl, ohv
Capacity	1.2 litres
Maximum power	54bhp
Chassis/suspension	Ladder chassis, semi-elliptic all round
Top speed	75mph
0–60mph	22.5 seconds

were perfectly matched to the engine performance – with a lovely slick change through a stubby little lever. The big instruments under the sweeping lines of the scuttle (with the rev counter set ahead of the driver and the speedometer set in front of the passenger!) told the TC driver everything he needed to know that he wasn't already feeling through the seat of his pants.

On such tall, narrow tyres it was quite exciting to throw a TC around on narrow lanes, the car compensating for its lack of outright grip by very forgiving manners and even a fairly comfortable ride for such a lightweight. It didn't have enough power to get into real trouble accidentally, but it did have enough to offer a controllable amount of oversteering fun.

Of course, if the driver really did want more, it was a very easy car to endow with more power and few TCs stayed completely standard for very long. Even with a tuned engine, the hydraulic drum brakes were quite good enough to stop the light little car solidly and with no more drama than a little wheel locking on a wet road – and if it *did* rain there was always a reasonably waterproof and easy to erect soft top on the outside and a rudimentary heater inside!

With its small, reliable engine and relatively simple engineering it cost very little to run or to repair, and, of course, when the sun shone (and usually even when it didn't) the top came off and the world was the TC owner's oyster.

The TC and the other T-series Midgets typified the MG name in particular on both sides of the Atlantic for almost 20 years, from the first TA of 1936 to the last TF of 1955 – and it will typify the sportscar ethic in general forever.

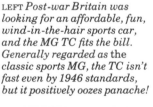

LEFT *Post-war Britain was looking for an affordable, fun, wind-in-the-hair sports car, and the MG TC fits the bill. Generally regarded as the classic sports MG, the TC isn't fast even by 1946 standards, but it positively oozes panache!*

BELOW *Long, low and sleek, the MG TC is a true two-seater sports car – there's little room for more than driver and passenger. For those less hardy souls, the TC comes as a convertible with heater. Luxury indeed!*

1951 ALLARD J2

Had Sydney Herbert Allard been alive today he would probably still be looking for the biggest, most powerful V8 he could find, then building the smallest possible amount of car to put it in. Allard died in April 1966, but at least he missed most of the frustration of seeing ever-increasing legislation shoving out the only sort of car he loved – simple, big-engined specials that were much bigger on character than on sophistication. Sophistication certainly was not Allard's forté, but he has to be respected for his unswerving conviction that anything, however unlikely, that made an Allard go faster was good. What made most Allards go faster was muscle – V8 muscle.

'The Guvnor', as he was always known, was a big, broad man who had started a garage business in South London in 1930 and quickly discovered the joys of the very English sport of trialling, with a modified Ford V8. In 1937 he started selling V8-powered specials, mostly for the mud-plugging trials but including a couple of road cars. He even built a few Lincoln V12-engined cars before World War II and, after the war, soon started building Ford V8 models again in fairly large numbers – some two-seaters, some four-seaters, a few drophead coupés and some short-chassis competition cars. In 1952 Allard won the Monte Carlo Rally in one of his own saloons, the only person ever to win driving his own make of car.

The Allard that everyone remembers, though, is

RIGHT *Allard lives! On the road or the racetrack, big is beautiful as far as Allards are concerned. This J2 model is powered by a 4.4 litre Mercury V-8 engine – getting the power down on to the road is helped by slinging a large fuel tank over the rear wheels.*

1950 ALLARD J2	
Engine	Mercury V8 ohv conversion
Capacity	4.3 litres
Maximum power	150bhp
Chassis/suspension	Ladder chassis, coil spring/lower arm ifs, De Dion rear
Top speed	120mph
0–60mph	—

the spectacular J2, a car that was equally successful on both sides of the Atlantic (as it was always planned to be) as a road car or a racer.

Allard competed with the first J2 at the famous Prescott hillclimb in the summer of 1949, winning his class in this 4.4-litre flathead Mercury V8-powered car. Unfortunately, because of postwar import problems, the J2 was generally restricted to flathead engines in Britain (albeit highly modified), so the real performance was reserved for the USA, where the choice of engine was almost boundless – a real paradise for Allard!

With overhead-valve Ford, Chrysler and Cadillac V8s (and sometimes with supercharging too) the J2 was a major success in America from its arrival in April 1950. Allard shipped rolling chassis with their good-looking, cycle-winged (fendered) aluminium bodies and left the customer to drop in whatever engine would fit.

The chassis could certainly handle it, with deep, stiff side rails and ample cross bracing. The front axle was a traditional Allard split-beam, but with coil springs, and the rear, also on coils, used a De Dion layout. The brakes too were especially good for their day, with big, hydraulically-operated drums all round.

Allard's way of ensuring enough traction for the more potent J2s included hanging a 40-gallon fuel tank over the back axle, and with maybe 300bhp in some cars it was needed – helping the quickest J2s to as much as 140mph/225kph. The racing J2X derivative was quicker still, capable of 150mph/241kph at Le Mans with full aerodynamic bodywork. With massive V8 torque in a car weighing little more than a ton it goes without saying that acceleration was spectacular even by today's standards.

Sadly, a car like the J2 could not last – even in the 1950s – there was just too much civilized competition from the likes of Jaguar beginning to appear. Ford dropped the V8 in Britain and Allard started looking at other projects by 1952 – but in 1981 the J2 re-appeared, built with 1950s character but 1980s running gear in Mississauga, Canada – by Allard's son!

1952 CUNNINGHAM C3 CONTINENTAL COUPÉ

Briggs Swift Cunningham was the epitome of the all-American millionaire sportsman. Born in 1907 into a substantial family fortune based on investments and stockholdings, he was a gifted track and field athlete in his college days who gave up his place in the 1929 US Olympic squad when he decided he was more interested in competitive sailing – and became a very capable yachtsman.

Eventually, his interests shifted again, this time to motor sports, which, like everything else, he pursued with a passion. Rich though he was, Cunningham would not go out and buy guaranteed success. A big part of the challenge would be in doing it himself, as a car constructor as well as just a driver – and in the big time, not the little league. He wanted to be a road racer European-style, rather than a track racer, and as well as building and racing his own cars he became actively involved in running the Automobile Racing

Club of America and its successor, the Sports Car Club of America.

He built his first car in 1940 and, at a time when it was fashionable to put American engines in European chassis, he did it the other way round, dropping a Mercedes engine into a stripped Buick to make the Bu-Merc.

The war put an end to that episode and Cunningham raced more conventional machinery, including MGs and Austin Healeys – plus the first Ferrari ever imported into the USA.

His interest in European racing and European cars was one thing, but his patriotism was another and he decided that he wanted to beat the Europeans at their own sportscar racing game, on home ground at Le Mans, with an all-American car.

His first entry (and the first American entry since 1935) was in 1950 with two Model 61 Cadillacs – one almost stock and the other with ugly 'streamlined' bodywork which earned it the nickname *le monstre*. They went well enough to make him pursue his Le Mans ambitions for many years, and from the later Le Mans project emerged a few roadgoing Cunningham sportscars, which might even have gone into serious production but for the pressures and expense of racing.

He started with the road car idea in 1951, planning to build Cunningham C2 production sportscars alongside the C1 racers in his new Palm Beach workshops. Four 1951 cars were built but only one was a road car, with a Cadillac V8, where the racers had Chrysler Hemis. One ran in second place at Le Mans before fuel problems pushed it back to 18th at the finish.

Cunningham even advertised his proposed road-going C2 derivatives late in 1951, as 'the ultimate in sportscars', but again he only built one, early in 1952, before Le Mans pressures took over again. More than ever though, he intended to build a road car and from February, 1952 he catalogued a 210bhp, 331cu in a Chrysler-powered, Vignale-bodied coupé, the C3 Continental.

It was fast, at almost 140mph/225kph but very, very expensive. A convertible, introduced in 1953, was even more expensive . . .

While the racing Cunninghams continued to give the Europeans an uncomfortably close run at Le Mans (with fourth place in 1952 and third in 1953), the Cunningham road cars sold just 18 coupés and nine convertibles before production petered out in 1955.

Briggs S, having for once failed to beat them, joined them – becoming Jaguar's US racing representative in 1956. He started his long association with Jaguar by using one of their engines in the 1957 C6RD Le Mans car – the last of the Cunninghams.

BELOW *American muscle versus the Europeans. Advertised as 'the ultimate in sportscars' the Cunningham C3 Continental Coupé was the road-going version of the racing cars built to challenge the likes of Jaguar at Le Mans.*

1952 CUNNINGHAM C3 CONTINENTAL COUPÉ	
Engine	Chrysler V8, ohv
Capacity	5.4 litres
Maximum power	210bhp
Chassis/suspension	Tubular chassis, coil spring/ wishbone ifs, De Dion rear
Top speed	138mph
0–60mph	—

1953 JAGUAR XK120

If ever one sportscar company truly lived up to the old adage of racing improving the breed, it is Jaguar. Through the 1950s Jaguar, with its C-Type and D-Type racing sportscars, took on the might of Ferrari and Mercedes-Benz at the highest levels of the sport, and frequently won – crowning its racing achievements with five Le Mans wins, including a hat-trick between 1955 and 1957.

The lessons of the racing Jaguars (most famously, disc brakes) were enthusiastically adopted for subsequent road cars and where Jaguar led, others followed. But the process really started in reverse, because the first great racing Jaguar, the C-Type, was actually developed from a Jaguar road car, the outstanding XK120 sports roadster.

The two-seater roadster version of the XK120 was introduced at the London Motor Show in 1948, rushed into what Jaguar envisaged as only limited production as a stop-gap model in which to introduce the company's new twin overhead camshaft XK-series engines – which were primarily intended for the forthcoming MkVII luxury saloon.

A four-cylinder XK100 was never put into production but the six-cylinder 3.4-litre XK120, with its beautifully sleek, modern lines, was the sensation of the show. Plans for a total run of 200 aluminium-bodied cars quickly gave way to full, steel-bodied production from 1949 and the XK line continued until the last XK150s of 1961 bowed out to the E-Type. The XK engine in various sizes was even longer lived, carrying over into the E-Type itself and into the saloon ranges; its basic layout is still instantly recognisable in six-cylinder Jaguars today.

As ever, the 120 part of the model designation represented Jaguar's top speed claim for the car – but in this case it was, if anything, a considerable understatement. A totally standard production model powered by the ultra-reliable 160bhp twin-carb engine was tested at the time at over 125mph/201kph. A works car, mildly tidied up aerodynamically, achieved almost 133mph/214kph and a later car, highly tuned and even more streamlined, recorded over 172mph/277kph in 1953.

The XK120 had roadholding to match its performance and looks, with a massive, cross-braced box-section chassis, independent torsion bar front suspension and semi-elliptic rear suspension. Ironi-

1953 JAGUAR XK120	
Engine	In-line, 6-cyl, 2ohv
Capacity	3.4 litres
Maximum power	160bhp
Chassis/suspension	Cross-braced, box-section, torsion bar ifs, semi-elliptic rear
Top speed	125mph
0–60mph	9.6 seconds

BELOW *Creating a motoring sensation with a stop-gap car. The Jaguar XK120 continued the theme of the SS100 with driveability and roadholding par excellence.*

RIGHT AND BELOW RIGHT *Modern sweeping lines of the XK120 were a revelation. The smooth six-cylinder engine used in the XK continued in production until 1986.*

cally, the only real weakness on the early XKs was the hydraulic drum brakes and after Jaguar had developed their disc system through the racing programme they were eventually transferred onto the later XK150s.

A fixed head coupé version of the XK120 was available from 1951 and a proper drophead coupé – as opposed to the original, rather spartan, roadster style – was introduced in 1953.

The XK120 was in production until 1954, when it was superseded by the more powerful but otherwise similar XK140. Over 12,000 120s were built and over 90 per cent were exported, around 60 per cent of them to the USA, where it firmly established Jaguar's reputation.

As well as amassing its own distinguished racing and rallying record, the XK120 also formed the basis in 1951 of the streamlined, tubular-framed C-Type, Jaguar's first out-and-out racing car. When Jaguar returned to Le Mans in the mid-1980s, they were looking to extend a record started when the C-Type won the 24-hour classic outright in 1951 and again in 1953. The C-Type might never have existed but for the popularity of the first XK120 show car.

1953 TRIUMPH TR2

T he Triumph TR2 is a wonderful example of how to make something out of nothing – or at least out of not very much: a cut-price classic from the corporate parts bin.

The TR part stands for Triumph Roadster, the name given to the first open-topped post World War II Triumph, which appeared in 1946 – shortly after the company had been taken over by Standard.

The Roadster, on a shortened 1800 saloon chassis, followed the lines of a one-off convertible built for the company's new chairman, Sir John Black; it was more of a well-equipped open tourer with sporting looks than a sportscar, but it had a lot to do with why Triumph wanted to be in the sportscar market.

Its original four-cylinder engine was the one that Standard had supplied to Jaguar's prewar predecessor, SS Cars. After World War II, Sir John Black, himself a great motoring enthusiast, wanted nothing more than to show Jaguar that he could build sports-

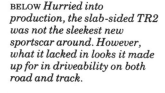

BELOW *Hurried into production, the slab-sided TR2 was not the sleekest new sportscar around. However, what it lacked in looks it made up for in driveability on both road and track.*

ABOVE RIGHT *The most inexpensive 100 mph sportscar on the market, the chunky body style of the TR2 enclosed mechanics borrowed from the Triumph saloon range to help keep costs down.*

cars too. He wanted to beat Jaguar and he wanted to beat MG, not least because he was well aware of the giant US market potential for a particular type of cheap and cheerful British sportscar.

He even tried to buy the Morgan company but failed and so he asked his engineers to come up, in a hurry, with a low-priced sportscar, based on available production parts. In six months they had a prototype ready for the 1952 London Motor Show, based on components largely from the 2-litre Standard Vanguard saloon – many of which were also used on the Ferguson tractor!

The car was well received and with a few months' refinement it re-emerged in mid-1953 as the production TR2.

The TR2 now had its own chassis, underslung at the rear, an engine linered-down to just under 2-litres (a competition class limit), gearbox and semi-elliptic rear axle also from the Vanguard, and front wishbone and coil spring suspension from Triumph's small 'razor-edge' saloon, the Mayflower.

Its chunkily-attractive slab-sided body also re-flected low tooling costs and hurried development, but somehow it all clicked and the little Triumph was a major success – as a racing and rally car as well as just in the showroom.

On 15-in wire wheels and quite narrow tyres, it handled well, if a little twitchily at the back, with a reasonable ride and a good level of comfort. It was well trimmed, acceptably roomy, and there was even a worthwhile boot (trunk) – even though the whole car had been built as small as possible to keep down material costs, weight and frontal area, the last two to help it to its target of 100mph/161kph performance.

It actually did its planned 100mph/161kph, in fact it could manage about 105mph/169kph, and at the time it was the cheapest 100mph/161kph car on the British market.

Most TR2s were not sold in their native Britain; of the 250 cars built in 1953, 200 were exported – almost all (no doubt to Sir John Black's delight) to the USA, where the TR quickly began to challenge the popularity of the suddenly dating T-series MGs as the 'in' sportscar.

From those small beginnings, production started properly in 1954 and over 8,600 TR2s were built up to 1955, which saw the arrival of the slightly more powerful and mildly restyled TR3, later to become the first British production car to use front-wheel disc brakes.

Through the TR3 and TR3A, the basic TR2 body shape survived for another six years; and so did its popularity, with more than 83,000 more examples being sold before the very different TR4 arrived in 1961 to start a new TR line.

1953 TRIUMPH TR2	
Engine	In-line, 4-cyl, ohv
Capacity	2.0 litres
Maximum power	90bhp
Chassis/suspension	Ladder chassis, coil spring/ wishbone ifs, semi-elliptic rear
Top speed	105mph
0–60mph	11.9 seconds

1954 PORSCHE 356 SPEEDSTER

Strictly speaking, the rear-engined layout, with the engine behind the gearbox, aft of the rear axle line, is a dubious configuration for any car, let alone a sportscar, which might reasonably be expected to be driven somewhere near its limits. So much weight concentrated so far back should inevitably make the tail want to wag the dog.

Yet Porsche, one of the most respected and successful of sportscar makers, has stuck doggedly to this contrary layout for almost 40 years, even persisting with it alongside more 'conventional' designs. Their current 911 types, even the enormously powerful Turbo, have the same basic configuration as the pro-

ABOVE *The mark of genius. Light and aerodynamic, the short-lived Porsche 356 Speedster uses the classic rear-engine configuration still used by Porsche to this day.*

duction 356 of 1948 – and there is no sign of Porsche abandoning it yet.

If, as has been said many times, the Porsche is a triumph of development over design, it is a triumph nonetheless.

The 356 was the first car to bear the Porsche name, though not the first to bear the stamp of Porsche's genius. Nominally, it was the 356th design of the Porsche design bureau, set up in Stuttgart in 1930. This was somewhat misleading, because Dr Porsche

1954 PORSCHE 356 'SPEEDSTER'	
Engine	A/c, flat 4-cyl
Capacity	1.3 litres
Maximum power	—
Chassis/suspension	Rear engined platform chassis, torsion bar independent
Top speed	120mph
0–60mph	10.0 seconds

started with Project 7, to avoid his first customers thinking he was inexperienced.

The first 356 prototype was based on Porsche's Berlin-Rome Axis Race streamliner of 1939, in turn based on the VW Beetle – which started life as Porsche Project 60 . . .

The 356 (designed by Dr Porsche's son Ferry to his father's brief, and completed in May 1948) had an open body and mid-engine (ahead of the gearbox and rear axle line), but all subsequent cars were rear-engined, to offer adequate cockpit space.

They used the platform chassis and all-torsion-bar trailing front/swing arm rear suspension of the Beetle, with a mildly tuned 40bhp version of the 1,131cc air-cooled flat-four Beetle engine.

Light weight and clean aerodynamics helped the car to a top speed of 85mph/137kph.

In August, 1948, Porsche completed the first 356 coupé and started small-scale production, launching the car officially early in 1949. Having built 50 cars in an interim workshop, Porsche got its Stuttgart works back from the US military in 1950 and started production in earnest.

The 356 developed rapidly, with the first capacity increase, to 1286cc, in 1951, followed by another, to 1582cc, in 1955 – this being the basic capacity until the last of the 356s in 1965. There was only one major body change, in 1959, with a larger windscreen and slight raising of the bumpers and headlamps, but there were many variations on the 356 theme, both open and closed.

One was the first Carrera; ultimately quickest of the 356s, in its 1965 130bhp 2-litre form, it took its name from the Carrera Panamericana, the Mexican road race in which Porsche won the small sportscar class at its first attempt in 1953. Porsche also won its class first time out at Le Mans, in 1951 with a racing coupé, quickly becoming a worldwide sales success too – especially on the west coast of the USA.

The most distinctive of all 356s was created for that market: the stunning but short-lived Speedster.

The Speedster, a sparsely equipped, lightweight, open 356 with a chopped down windscreen, clearly evoked the racing image. It had near racing performance too, with a 120mph/193kph top speed, 10-second 0–60mph/96.5kph times and superb brakes and transmission. Whatever people said about Porsche handling, very few cars could pass one.

It was introduced in 1954 after American importer Max Hoffman had bought a racing Spyder and mooted the lookalike to Porsche. It was dropped fairly quickly when Porsche realised they could not possibly make money on such a basic car however many they sold.

There are some miracles that even Porsche cannot work . . .

1955 MERCEDES-BENZ 300SL

The gull-winged Mercedes-Benz 300SL is one of the most distinctive of all sportscars. Outstandingly successful on both road and track, it was pioneering in many ways, though some of its most striking features were pure compromise. Yet it remains one of the greatest of all sporting classics.

It started life as a racing model, when three cars (including a little used open example) were built for the 1952 season. This was Mercedes' first racing effort after World War II and the budget by their standards was tiny.

Logically enough, the 300SL was designed around Mercedes' biggest production engine – a 3-litre straight-six, introduced in 1951 and then used in the big, 110mph/177kph 300S saloon.

300SL stood for 3-litre *Sport-Leicht*, or light sportscar, and light was the key word. The engine was big and heavy so the rest of the car had to be as light as possible, to which end the competition department designed a frighteningly complicated, stressed multi-tubular spaceframe, which weighed little more than 110lb. To this they bolted coil spring front suspension, swinging arm rear suspension and an aluminium coupé body with the famous gullwing doors. It was their only reasonable option, as the chassis had to be so deep in the sills to achieve the desired stiffness that conventional doors were out of the question.

To keep the bonnet (hood) line low the engine was canted through 40° *and* offset to one side.

Among its four major racing successes in its first year was a win at Le Mans – which every sportscar manufacturer still recognises as the one motor racing event with truly worldwide impact.

It was Mercedes' New York agent who suggested turning the 300SL into a road car and when the company expressed doubts he eased their uncertainty with a firm order for 1,000 cars!

The first production prototype was unveiled at the New York Auto Show in February, 1954 and production proper started in August. The road car looked very similar to the racing original, save for a few styling bulges and a different headlamp arrangement, but it had several major differences.

Most of the body (except the slightly larger doors, the boot (trunk) and bonnet (hood)) were steel, and the interior was fully trimmed – though it retained

LEFT *Probably the most famous Mercedes of all-time, the gull-wing 300SL is race-bred. 140 mph/224 kph and stunning acceleration are combined with somewhat treacherous handling – not a car for the faint-hearted.*

LEFT AND RIGHT *Wearing its three-pointed star with pride. Super-sleek styling and hand-built craftsmanship combine to make the 300SL look right from every angle.*

the tilting steering wheel which made entry merely difficult rather than totally impossible.

Where the Le Mans engine had used carburettors, production engines pioneered the use of Bosch direct fuel injection, and all road engines were also dry-sumped.

Although the road car was substantially heavier than the racer, and slower, it was still streets ahead of any opposition. With 195bhp (or an optional 215) it was good for maybe 140mph/225kph, and up to 228lb ft of torque gave instant pulling power from as little as 15mph/24kph in top gear. On the lowest of three optional axle ratios it would reach 60mph/96.5kph in under 7½ seconds and 100mph/161kph in less than 15 seconds.

The chassis was a mixture of good and bad; the huge aluminium-finned drum brakes, with servo-assistance, were exceptional, but the swinging arm rear suspension gave the sort of high speed oversteer that only a really gifted driver could cope with. On the newly fashionable radial tyres, it was especially

difficult . . .

In 1957, the gullwing was replaced (after 1,400 had been hand-built) by a roadster – largely on the strength of the Californian market. It had lower sills and conventional doors, plus many other refinements – notably to the rear suspension – which gave it better manners but not nearly so much character. Although it sold 1,858 copies by 1963, it will inevitably be remembered only as the mighty gullwing's lesser cousin.

1955 MERCEDES-BENZ 300 SL	
Engine	In-line, 6-cyl, sohc
Capacity	3.0 litres
Maximum power	195bhp
Chassis/suspension	Multi-tubular spaceframe, coil spring ifs, swinging arm irs
Top speed	140mph
0–60mph	7.5 seconds

1956 CHEVROLET CORVETTE

In America in the mid-1950s, auto industry engineers and stylists were a lot more interested in building sportscars than the public was in buying them. The few odd-balls who did want open-top two-seaters either bought European or went to the small but expensive specialist builders like Kurtis and Cunningham. To the Big Three they were a weird minority, not a potential profit area. Not, that is, until General Motors took the plunge with the Corvette – a nameplate which has survived ever since as the all-time biggest selling American sports-car.

Of all manufacturers, GM had perhaps the best idea of what people would buy in the future, gauged largely through what extravagances they could get away with in their annual Motorama showcars.

That was how the Corvette idea began. With the arrival of the new generation overhead-valve V8s in the early 1950s, America was quick to come to terms with horsepower, but GM was undoubtedly surprised by the enthusiastic reaction to the Corvette prototype which the Chevrolet Division showed at the 1953 Motorama.

It was a thoroughly European two-seater, far smaller than anything GM might reasonably have expected to gain public approval; and far from having all the trimmings of the typical showcar, it was basic in the extreme. It was so small because the engineers had ignored convention and designed it that way, placing all the major components as close together as they would go, and it looked so good because they had entrusted the fibreglass bodyshell to master-stylist Harley Earl.

So loud was the cheering for the Corvette that GM decided to plunge straight into production – intending to use fibreglass for the first 300 cars to give them time to tool into metal. They never had to – the public accepted the new material, production methods were refined and America's first mass-produced sportscar stayed plastic.

Given this open-armed enthusiasm, it is amazing how close GM came to getting the Corvette totally wrong. It was launched in 1953 with a 150bhp version of the elderly 235cu in the Chevy Six and the stodgy auto that went with it. GM had had a late attack of conservatism and aimed the Corvette mid-market. Its excellent chassis and sporty looks became

1956 CHEVROLET CORVETTE	
Engine	V8, ohv
Capacity	4.3 litres
Maximum power	225bhp
Chassis/suspension	Perimeter frame, coil spring/ wishbone ifs, semi-elliptic rear
Top speed	120mph
0–60mph	7.5 seconds

an embarrassment when big, gin-palace-trimmed sedans with gutsy V8s could wallow by on any decent straight stretch.

What saved the Corvette was the 1955 option of the new and brilliant 265 Chevy V8 and a 1956 restyling. The result was equally spectacular looks *and* performance. With options up to 225bhp, the milestone 1956 Corvette became an outstanding car, well capable of over 120mph/193kph and 0–60mph/96.5kph in just 7½ seconds. Tuned for racing, a 1955 Corvette would touch 150mph/241kph and racing development further improved the already good production chassis. With the arrival of a three-speed, close ratio manual gearbox, superbly balanced handling and refined horsepower, the 1956 Corvette was a sportscar worthy of any company.

It was just a little too late for the boom sales year of 1955, and just a bit too expensive at over $3,100, but it had now become so good that Corvette sales soon far exceeded anything Chevrolet had ever envisaged back in 1953.

The Corvette became an American institution. It gained bigger and better V8s over the years and changed dramatically with the arrival of the Stingray in 1963. The 1956 Corvette probably remains America's closest approach to the universal sportscar, though Corvettes since have continued to be outstanding.

RIGHT *Corvette – the all-American sportscar. Compact by American standards, the Corvette sports a fibreglass bodyshell powered by a Chevy V-8 engine. A superbly-engineered chassis endows the car with razor-sharp handling. In road trim, a Corvette would reach 120 mph/192 kph – racing versions were good for another 30 mph/48 kph.*

1956 FORD THUNDERBIRD

In 1951, Ford's Vice President, Lewis Crusoe, and his assistant, George Walker, looked around the Paris Salon at the proliferation of Ferraris, Porsches and Jaguars and decided, there and then, that a sportscar was just what Ford needed to bolster its badly jaded image. Walker, a freelance designer, called his own studio and by the time the two of them arrived back in the USA his staff had already drawn up the outline of what would become the Thunderbird.

Although the Ford management quickly agreed to the idea, the company's dire financial problems committed them to building their sportscar on the cheap. It was planned as a fairly lightweight two-seater with soft-top and V8 power. The catch was that it had to use as many existing Ford parts as possible and it had to happen quickly – to give Ford a competitor for the newly launched Chevrolet Corvette.

The good news was that the Ford stylists, who were traditionally poor relations to the engineers, were given an unusually free hand – including a good deal of cooperation with the mechanical layout. Early tests were carried out using a shortened sedan chassis, with relatively soft suspension, but the T'bird's own chassis and running gear, with the engine set lower down and further back just as the stylists had asked, was developed in parallel.

The first prototype, early in 1954, already looked wonderful – low, sleek and largely free of the usual flashiness, but it was too heavy. Conveniently, Ford was able to take a quick look at the sales problems of the early Corvettes and chicken out of calling the Thunderbird a sportscar. Not only did they not have to go on an expensive and time consuming crash diet but they felt free to load on even more weight, in the form of an optional hardtop and power everything, thereby upgrading the Thunderbird to what Ford dubbed a 'personal car'.

As such, the Thunderbird went on sale, with the soft-top now optional, in October, 1954. At $2,695 it was even cheaper than the spartan six-cylinder Corvette and not surprisingly it outsold the early Chevy quite handsomely – by more than twenty to one in 1955, with over 16,000 sales.

The best of the T'birds was generally reckoned to be the 1956 model, which was still as near as made no odds to a sportscar, whatever Ford chose to call it. It

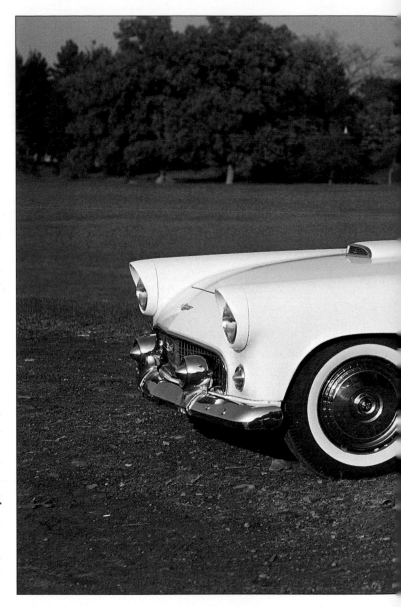

had put right the few problems of the earlier cars but actually changed very little. Even so, it was the most distinguishable of all Thunderbirds, with a one-year-only adoption of a 'continental' spare wheel location (vertically at the rear) and optional portholes in the rear quarters of the hardtop. It used a 202bhp version of Ford's 292cu in V8 and manual transmission as standard, with the 312cu in V8 as an option.

With softer rear springs and lower geared steering than the earlier examples its handling was less

1956 FORD THUNDERBIRD	
Engine	V8, ohv
Capacity	4.8 litres
Maximum power	202bhp
Chassis/suspension	Cross-braced ladder chassis, coil spring/wishbone ifs, semi-elliptic
Top speed	115mph
0–60mph	9.5 seconds

BELOW *Stylish competition for the Corvette, the Ford Thunderbird went upmarket with 'power-assisted*

everything'. A sports car in everything but name, the Thunderbird has become a legend.

twitchy and the good looking car would reach around 115mph/185kph, with 60mph/96.5kph coming up in under ten seconds. As such it lagged a little way behind the contemporary Corvette (now with the V8 it always needed) in everything but sales – but with the Chevy rapidly gaining ground to cut the margin to about three to one.

Ironically, that reflected a complete reversal of roles; the Corvette, which had started out as a mid-market car, had turned into a real sportscar, while the T'bird, which should have been a sportscar, had softened up into a 'personal' car.

The reversal continued, with the Thunderbird turning into an ordinary four-seater only a year or so later and the Corvette beating it in both sales and performance terms.

Maybe Americans really did want a sportscar in the 1950s, after all. It would not be the first time that the American market had been misjudged by a major American manufacturer.

1957 LOTUS 7 (CATERHAM 7)

The Caterham Super Seven has often been described as the nearest thing to a motorcycle on four wheels, and that is probably still the best description there can be for this extraordinary car – which has been around with few fundamental changes since 1957!

It was launched as the Lotus Seven, a kit-built sportscar designed by Colin Chapman, the genius behind Lotus and a man well known for his absolute refusal to compromise.

There was certainly no compromise about the Seven. It was, and is, an out-and-out sportscar with absolutely no pretensions to being anything else. It has two seats and virtually no luggage space, rudimentary weather protection in the guise of an awkward-to-erect hood and side screens (which, when up, make getting in and out virtually impossible), and very few other creature comforts. However, it does have a race-bred tubular chassis and suspension which contribute to roadholding and

handling well beyond all normal realms – and with any of the vast choice of engines which have been available over the years, and barely half-ton of car has a blistering straightline performance. With any of the more potent engine options it will nudge six seconds for the dash to 60mph/96.5kph – even though its top speed is limited by the aerodynamics. Impressively, it achieves all this for no more than the cost of a sporty hatchback and combines its performance with a style as individual as anything on the road.

Everything about the Seven flatters the enthusiastic driver: beautifully precise controls; strictly functional instruments and trim; even the laid-back driving position which is so exhilaratingly close to the road. Barring a few aesthetic drawbacks, driving the Caterham Super Seven is a pure joy.

Over the years, engine options grew from small pushrod units, through Formula Ford type units, the famous Lotus Twincam in various stages of tune, to that engine's modern replacement, the big-valve,

LEFT BELOW *Four-wheeled motorbike? The thoroughly individual Caterham 7 pays no heed to modern comforts. The basic design of the car hasn't changed since 1957 – it's fast, it's fun and it's oh so impractical!*

BELOW *Light-weight body and powerful engine add up to true supercar performance. Limpet-like grip and phenomenal levels of handling complement the blistering acceleration.*

1957 LOTUS 7 (CATERHAM 7)	
Engine	In-line, 4-cyl, ohv
Capacity	1690cc
Maximum power	135bhp
Chassis/suspension	Tubular space frame, aluminium-clad ifs, live axle rear
Top speed	112mph
0–60mph	5.6 seconds

twin-cam built for Caterham by Lotus preparation specialists Vegantune.

In the early days, almost all Sevens were sold in kit form to take advantage of a British tax concession of the time, but in 1973 that exemption was withdrawn, putting prices up substantially and all but killing the Seven. Where many other specialist cars were prematurely buried because of this, the Seven survived.

It was saved by a long-time Lotus dealer, Caterham Cars, in Surrey, who acquired production rights (though not use of the Lotus name) from Lotus in May 1973 and have been producing the car, with constant improvements, ever since.

Although Caterham actually took over the angu-lar, fibreglass-bodied Series 4 car (which Lotus had only recently introduced) customer opinion soon persuaded them to revert to the classic, alloy-panelled, fibreglass-nosed and -winged Series 3 design which survives today.

In 1982 Caterham added a long-cockpit option to give bigger drivers a touch more leg-room but neither that nor the myriad engine and chassis variations have changed the essential character of the Super Seven in the slightest. On a warm summer's day and an open road the Seven still offers about as much fun as it is possible to have in any road car at any price, which is quite an achievement for a car that started out as a kit!

1961 JAGUAR E-TYPE

By 1961, Jaguar were used to having their new cars acclaimed as 'sensational'. In the 1920s, their Swallow-bodied forerunners were seen as the essence of style; in the 1930s the SS100 offered unbeatable performance for its price; in 1948 the XK120 combined speed, style and amazing value for money; and in the 1950s the racing D-Types beat the world. But none of them caused the same sensation as the exquisite E-Type, unveiled in March, 1961 at the Geneva Show. Its incredible looks, world-beating performance and almost unbelievably low price instantly rendered all its mass-produced contemporaries also-rans.

The E-Type's relationship with the D-Type showed quite clearly both above and below the surface. The sleek shape was very much like a longer, lower D-Type and had actually started to evolve as early as 1953 on an interim car between the C- and D-Types. A fastback coupé was offered alongside the roadster and, of course, all the E-Types were much better equipped than the spartan, racing Ds.

Under the skin, the new car had the familiar central monocoque with tubular subframes at front and rear, but, for the first time, Jaguar used an all-independent suspension. The front was based on wishbones and torsion bars; the clever new rear arrangement housed the final drive (with its inboard

disc brakes) in a frame attached to the rear of the monocoque, fixed length driveshafts acted as a top link, and there were wide-based lower wishbones and radius arms – all controlled by two big coil spring damper units at each side.

It worked brilliantly and the layout is still essentially unchanged on all Jaguars today, including the nearest thing to a sportscar, the V12 engined XJ-S Cabriolet.

Both open and closed E-Types, powered by the 265bhp 3.8-litre triple carb XK twin-cam engine, would do as near 150mph/241kph as made no difference – the coupé perhaps 1mph more, the less aerodynamic drophead (for which a detachable hardtop was available) perhaps 1mph under. Both could reach 60mph/96.5kph in seven seconds and return a respectable 20mpg/14lp100km – thanks to their exceptional aerodynamics and acceptably light weight.

Handling and roadholding were superb, letting even the ordinary driver enjoy much of the extraordinary performance; but the E-Type did have its faults. The earliest cars were quite cramped; they tended to overheat; the faired-in headlamps were hopeless (they were changed in 1967 for new US regulations); the all-disc brakes were marginal for such performance; and the early gearboxes were dreadfully slow and heavy.

Jaguar overcame most problems very quickly, ironically because they had again totally underestimated demand and had only planned a limited run! They cured many faults simply by going into proper tooling.

And, of course, the E-Type developed over the years anyway – though not always for the better.

The first cars were never surpassed for outright performance, with later power increases always offset by added weight. In 1964 the E-Type was given a 4.2-litre engine and an excellent new all-syncro gearbox. In 1966 the less attractive, high-roofed, long wheelbase 2+2 was introduced, with an automatic gearbox option. The car adapted to new US regulations in the late 1960s but the biggest change came in 1970 when Jaguar launched its magnificent 5.3-litre V12 engine in the E-Type, replacing the XK sixes.

This 272bhp engine, still considered one of the finest in the world, brought the E-Type a new refinement and a very different image – as a grand tourer rather than an outright sportscar.

E-Type production continued until early 1975, by which time more than 72,500 had been built, including some 15,000 V12s.

The XJ-S which replaced it was even less of a sportscar than the last E-Type. Even for Jaguar, the original E-Type was a very hard act to follow.

1961 JAGUAR E-TYPE	
Engine	In-line, 6-cyl, 2ohc
Capacity	3.8 litres
Maximum power	265bhp
Chassis/suspension	Central monocoque, tubular sub-frames, torsion bar ifs, coil spring irs
Top speed	150mph
0–60mph	7.0 seconds

BELOW *Cat that got the cream. The E-type Jaguar is* the *sportscar of the 1960s.*

1962 AC COBRA

1965 AC COBRA 427	
Engine	Ford V8, ohv
Capacity	7 litres
Maximum power	425bhp
Chassis/suspension	Tubular ladder, coil spring suspension all round
Top speed	160mph
0–60mph	4.5 seconds

The AC Cobra was an Anglo-american hybrid which actually worked, and the final fling of the no-holds-barred sportscar before the Ralph Nader era put a stop to such overt overkill. After Nader's book *Unsafe At Any Speed* (Grossman, New York, 1965) was published and the 'consumer protection' lobby grew, motoring in America and around the world changed dramatically. Gone was the hey-day of the musclecar, the horsepower race and the open top; in came downsizing, detoxing and crash testing; and out went cars like the Cobra with its big engine in a lightweight chassis, massive performance, open top and all. Happily, the Cobra had already guaranteed its own immortality as one of the fastest, most evocative sportscars of any era.

It evolved from 1961, when American racing driver Carroll Shelby took his version of the 'US engine/European chassis' idea to AC Cars in Britain. He had already been turned down by Aston Martin (even though he had won Le Mans for them in 1959), Jensen and Maserati, but he timed his arrival at AC perfectly – just as they were looking for more power for their excellent 2.6-litre Ford-powered Ace chassis.

By September, 1961 the project was under way. Ford, committed to its image-building 'total performance' programme, saw Shelby's idea as a way to pull buyers into Ford showrooms and responded to his approaches by giving him two of their latest 221cu in V8s to work with. The first example of what Shelby dubbed the Cobra ran in Britain in January, 1962, before several chassis, based on the Ace but much stronger, were shipped to the USA to be fitted with engines – which by then had grown to 260cu in.

Where others had failed, the Cobra triumphed, combining exceptional straightline performance with the handling and braking that AC always knew their chassis could provide. Shelby arranged to sell the cars through Ford dealers in the USA and the first 100 were commissioned late in 1962 in an effort to qualify the Cobra for international racing.

Late in 1962 the Cobra lost its inboard rear disc brakes but gained the classic 271bhp 289cu in Ford V8, to become the Mark II – sold in America as the Shelby Ford Cobra. This 289 Cobra was already indecently quick, giving -second 0–60 times and a 000mph top speed, but there was much more to come.

BELOW AND RIGHT *The immortal AC Cobra (here in 7-litre form) is amazingly quick by any standards. The massive V8 in the lightweight body will propel the Cobra to 60 mph/96 kph in 4½ seconds and on to a maximum of 160 mph/256 kph!*

Racing was part of the Cobra's *raison d'etre* and it was obviously capable, with modification, of coping with considerably more horsepower. One product of Ford's NASCAR sedan racing programme was the famous 427 engine, which in 'standard' form gave some 425bhp. Shelby soon adopted it as a way to challenge the big Corvettes in American sportscar racing, allowing the Cobra to dominate for several years.

Derivatives, including the Daytona coupé which appeared in 1964, were very successful in international racing, just missing the world endurance championship in 1964 before becoming the first ever American winner of the World Manufacturers' Championship for GT cars in 1965.

In January, 1965 the staggeringly quick 427 (typically capable of 160mph/257kph and 12-second standing quarters) was launched as a road car. Ford had helped design new coil spring suspension and a stronger chassis but some of the 427's straightline muscle ws compromised by less agile handling than the 289.

The leaf-sprung chassis was dropped when the 427 arrived but AC put 289 engines into the later chassis as the AC 289 Mark III – and some cars were made with the cheaper 355bhp 'police special' 428 engine from the Ford Galaxie.

However, *every* Cobra was a classic, some just more than others. Only post-Nader legislation and consumer activists could beat the Cobra and production stopped in 1967. The Cobra lives on though – in 1982, with AC's approval, the British company Autocraft began to make genuine AC Mark IVs on the original 427 jigs. Perhaps the American enthusiasts will be able to enjoy the Cobra again, this time an imported version.

1964 AUSTIN HEALEY 3000 MkIII

They were affectionately called the 'Big Healeys', by almost everyone, and the Austin Healey 3000s really were larger-than-life in many respects – almost the end of the line for macho sportscars, before brute force, sadly, became less than socially acceptable.

The family line started in 1952 when specialist car builder Donald Healey exhibited his open, two-seater Healey 100 at the London Motor Show. Powered by a 2.6-litre four-cylinder engine derived from the big Austin A90 saloon and with a straghtforward ladder chassis and simply running gear, it attracted the approval of BMC management. They were looking for just such a sportscar, which they could build cheaply around existing Austin parts and fill what they saw as a yawning market gap between the small MGs and Triumphs and the bigger, more specialized Jaguars. They soon came to an agreement with Healey and his car went into production in 1953 as the Austin Healey 100, with a top speed of 102mph/164kph. The bodies were built by another specialist sportscar maker, Jensen, whose own 1952 Motor Show design had also impressed BMC, but not quite so much as the Healey.

The four-cylinder cars, including the tuned 100S, which started a distinguished competition career for the Healeys, were built until 1956, when a 102bhp six-cylinder 2.6-litre engine was introduced. In a slightly longer, slightly heavier but still very similar looking shell (mainly different in offering a token passenger space behind the front seats), this became known as the 100-6. It carried on the tradition of good performance with few frills and continued to sell in large numbers – almost all earning valuable export income.

In 1959 the car underwent a fairly major revision, with some chassis strengthening, front disc brakes and a capacity increase to 2.9 litres, to emerge as the Austin Healey 3000.

With power up to 124bhp from a triple-carburettor engine, the 3000 gave an even more vivid performance, with a top speed of about 116mph/187kph and predictably impressive low-speed flexibility.

In 1961 a MkII version was introduced with 132bhp and in 1964 the definitive MkIII appeared, now with only two carbs but with power up to 148bhp, for a top speed of 123mph/198kph and quite brutal

1964 AUSTIN HEALEY 3000 MK III	
Engine	In-line, 6-cyl, ohv
Capacity	2.9 litres
Maximum power	148bhp
Chassis/suspension	Cross-braced ladder coil spring/ wishbone ifs, semi-elliptic rear
Top speed	123mph
0–60mph	—

LEFT BELOW *The engine of this Austin Healey 3000, sports a triple-SU carburettor set-up. In this form the straight-six engine puts out 132 bhp.*

acceleration in the lower gears. Such refinements as wind-up windows and new walnut dash trim did nothing to change the uncompromising muscularity of the beast at all – which was a good thing.

Certainly the Big Healey had some shortcomings. Though capable of being docile, and with its overdrive gearing quite relaxed at speed, the brakes were heavy, it was a brute to drive hard, short on driver space (especially around the pedals), shorter still on luggage space, and the seats belied their comfortable looks. Regardless of any complaints, the 3000 built an exceptional reputation as a rally car. The famous red and white, alloy-bodied, 210bhp works cars scored literally dozens of major victories – including the 1964 Alpine Rally and two Liège–Sofia–Liège Rallies – and it was a successful circuit racer in its class for many years.

It lasted until the end of 1967, and of the 43,000 cars built, well over 90 per cent were exported.

BELOW *True Brit – the ultimate 'Big Healey' – the Mk III was good for around 125 mph/200 kph. 3000s notched up many rally successes. High-speed cruising was no problem, but fast hard driving required plenty of muscle!*

1964 FORD MUSTANG

Ford has a longstanding habit of getting it right, and this was exemplified by the Mustang, the original pony-car. In its early days at least, the Mustang was much closer to being a sportscar than most Americans had ever thought they would buy. But buy it they did, in their millions.

For Ford, it was a calculated change of image from conservative to glamorous and a change of market from middle age to youth – aimed right at the millions who had grown up, with money in their pockets, from the postwar baby boom.

It emerged at the time of Ford's 'total performance' programme and America's growing awareness of the smaller, sportier European cars. The Mustang, like 'total performance', was dreamed up by the young, go-ahead new boss of the Ford Division, Lee Iacocca – now boss of Chrysler. The Mustang I was a 1962 mid-engined two-seater show car, but was never intended for production. The first *real* Mustang, thoroughly conventional but with the elusive spark of style, was seen in April 1964 at the New York World's Fair. Within hours of the car going on sale in the same month, Ford's $65 million development and $10 million advertising investments began to look like the best money they had ever spent.

Every available car was sold during that first day and orders taken for over 20,000 more.

What everyone wanted was a rakish four-seater, on a 108-in wheelbase, that Ford's in-house stylists had carefully contrived to look like a sporty two-seater. It was available as a hard-top or a convertible with engine options from a gutless 170cu in six, through a 260cu in V8 (derived like most of the rest of the Mustang's running gear from the Fairlane) to a 164bhp 289cu in V8 – plus manual or auto transmissions.

BELOW *Mustang-pony-car for a new generation. Clever marketing by Ford made the rakishly-styled Mustang an overnight success. Steve McQueen drove a Mustang to fame in the now legendary car chase scene in the film* Bullitt.

1965 FORD MUSTANG	
Engine	V8, ohv
Capacity	4.7 litres
Maximum power	271bhp
Chassis/suspension	Platform chassis, coil spring ifs, semi-elliptic rear
Top speed	121mph
0–60mph	8.1 seconds

It was offered at a rock-bottom basic price with minimal equipment but could be loaded up with a vast assortment of profit generating options – and most buyers did load up. Those unable to shrug off old habits went for the autos, but few took the 101bhp six.

With Ford struggling to keep up with demand, especially for the V8s, sales passed 100,000 within four months. They passed a quarter of a million well before the end of 1964 (by which time the smaller six had been dropped and the GT 2+2 'fastback' option added) and the first million within two years.

The Mustang was more than just another car, it was a phenomenon, the fastest selling new car ever and Ford's floodgate to the new generation.

Ford had no hesitation in those less fettered days in selling performance. Options, on top of the power-train choices, included harder suspension (by coils at the front and cart springs at the rear), bigger wheels, higher geared steering and better brakes – all of which the car really needed as standard!

The Mustang could not attain *real* European standards but it was a genuinely sporty car by prevailing American standards, with its bucket seats and floor gearshift.

For a while, the Mustang forged ahead, sharpening up its reflexes and growing in potency – with the early 270bhp Cobra-engined versions good for 120mph/193kph and sub-16-second standing quarters. But then it began to grow out of the simplicity which gave it instant appeal but negligible basic profit margins. By 1967 it was bigger and by 1969, when the Mach I was introduced, it had lost most of its original character. Engine options peaked with the 429cu in 'Boss' engine and 375bhp but no version since has been as close to a real sportscar as the classic original.

1964 LOTUS ELAN

If you believe that what really makes a sportscar is *fun* then this is where you can stop looking. Some sportscars are technically brilliant, some are historically important, several are staggeringly quick. The Lotus Elan is the one with everything. It doesn't have the outright performance of a Ferrari or a Lamborghini, but it doesn't have the pricetag either. It doesn't have the breeding or the name of a Bentley or a Bugatti, but it doesn't have *either* the pricetag or the ever-present responsibility of driving a piece of history. It doesn't always have the reliability of something as mundane as an MG or a Jaguar, but it does have twice the character.

On a sunny summer's afternoon, with the top down and nowhere special to go, it doesn't even have *quite* the raw entertainment of the equally cheap and even less conventional Seven, but if it rains and you're carrying more than a toothbrush and a towel it will get you there reasonably dry and uncrumpled and your luggage (not too much of it, mind you) won't have to come on behind.

It has its faults; if you drive one the way it cries out to be driven you might spend almost as much time underneath it as in it – a small price to pay. The air conditioning involves no more than taking the top down; the only in-car-entertainment is in driving it. Before General Motors took over Lotus early in 1986, Lotus was planning a small, cheap, mass-produced sportscar. Everybody, but everybody, dubbed it 'an Elan for the 'eighties'.

The Elan for the 'sixties (and into the early 'seventies) was a compact, fibreglass-bodied drophead (or, later, coupé) two-seater, powered by various versions of the Ford-based Lotus twin-cam engine. It was shown first at the London Motor Show late in 1962, but didn't reach production until early 1963. Production then didn't necessarily mean complete assembly; a British tax concession of the time (a loophole if you prefer) said that cars bought as 'kits' escaped purchase tax. Lotus was one of many specialist car makers to take advantage of leaving the wheels off and engine out, but was one of the few to survive when the concession disappeared in 1973.

The Elan is a wonderfully simple car. It introduced the classic Lotus backbone chassis, forked at the front to carry the legendary four-cylinder twin-cam engine and coil spring and wishbone suspension, and less markedly at the back to take a Chapman strut with wide-based lower wishbones and rubber-jointed driveshafts.

The original 1½-litre motor gave 100bhp but only a few were made before the classic 105bhp 1.6-litre unit was introduced, the original engines being recalled and replaced, free of charge. As ever, the bottom-line power grew over the years, with up to 126bhp on offer from 1971 in Sprint versions. There were other changes, like a fixed-head coupé from 1965 and even a slightly bigger +2 sister model from 1967, but they were all Elans.

In many ways, the early ones were the best, like first thoughts, or first impressions. The fibreglass-reinforced plastic body, with its neat pop-up headlamps, never changed much (save for the obvious hardtop and +2 variants) and the biggest first-glance differences between early and late Elans are gradually increasing tyre widths and a bonnet (hood) bulge on the third series.

It is easy to feel at home in an Elan; functional design was Chapman's immutable creed. The car is only just over 12ft/3m long and knee-high, but it is amazingly comfortable even for the biggest driver. Everything works; the stubby gearlever flicks from ratio to ratio just like a switch, the handling is as sharp as a kart on rails and the all-round disc brakes simply stop the car on demand. The balance between soft springs and firm damping give a sweet ride in spite of the low weight and the actual grip would frighten almost any car in the world: point the Elan at corners and it goes round them; simple as that. It won't do more than 110mph/176kph (say 125/200kph with the best engine and more aerodynamic hardtop) but on an average road it will run rings round cars 50mph/80kph faster and ten times the price.

It isn't the *greatest* sportscar in the word perhaps, but if an Elan doesn't tell you what a *real* sportscar is, nothing will.

RIGHT *Colin Chapman had a flair for putting life into his cars, and perhaps none more so than his Lotus Elan. Functional in design and layout, the Elan combines simplicity with leech-like roadholding and a willing (if occasionally unreliable) twin-cam engine.*

1964 LOTUS ELAN	
Engine	In-line, 4-cyl, 2ohc
Capacity	1.6 litres
Maximum power	105bhp
Chassis/suspension	Backbone, coil spring/wishbone ifs, coil spring/Chapman strut irs
Top speed	110mph
0–60mph	8.7 seconds

1966 FORD GT40

Of all the glories that 'total performance' achieved for Ford in the 1960s, perhaps the greatest was not the run of Le Mans wins, or Indianapolis, or even the incalculable spin-off value of vastly increased sales, but one exceptional car – a road car as well as a Le Mans winner – the immortal GT40.

The GT40 was the true measure of how seriously Ford took its racing programme, the car that had to beat Ferrari at the highest levels of sportscar competition. It was an affair of honour; when Ford identified Le Mans as the one and only prize that would bring *worldwide* recognition it tried initially not to beat Ferrari but to buy it. The result would have been Ford-Ferrari road cars and Ferrari-Ford racing cars, but in the end Ford's $15 million offer was not enough to overcome Ferrari's fierce independence and pride.

Instead, in 1963, Ford, with a lot of help from the British racing car manufacturer Lola, began to develop the GT40. Lola had shown a Ford V8 powered, mid-engined GT racing car early in 1963 and that was the car around which Ford's development contract was negotiated. The gestation of the GT40 (named for its planned height of just 40in) was extremely short and in April 1964 the first car was shipped to the USA.

It had the 256cu in, all-alloy, pushrod V8 from the 1963 Indianapolis programme, giving about 350bhp and a theoretical maximum speed of close to 200mph/322kph. There were a few teething problems and in fact it took Ford until 1966 to win its coveted first Le Mans, the GT40 having won only two major races up to the end of 1965!

By then the GT40 had grown into the Mark II from early 1965, with 427 V8 power derived from the NASCAR Fords, de-tuned to 'only' 427bhp for endurance racing. Ford Advanced Vehicles in Britain

1967 FORD GT40 (ROAD)	
Engine	V8, ohv
Capacity	4.2 litres
Maximum power	350bhp
Chassis/suspension	Steel monocoque, independent coil spring/wishbone all round
Top speed	165mph
0–60mph	5.0 seconds

RIGHT *The GT40 was developed with one aim in mind – to win the Le Mans 24 Hour Race and beat Ferrari. And win they did, not just once, but four times in a row. Roadgoing GT40s are little different to the racing versions – performance is positively shattering with a 5-seconds 0–60 mph/0–96 kph time.*

also began to build 289cu in GT40s in some numbers from mid-1965, and even built some open cars that year. In all, about 120 GT40s and their derivatives were built and as well as the hugely successful racing types (which went on to win Le Mans four times in a row) Ford also offered genuine roadgoing GT40s, and sold about 31 road cars by 1967.

The first road cars used a 335bhp version of the 289 V8, to give a top speed of 164mph/264kph – with 127mph/204kph in second gear, 142mph/228.5kph in third and 142mph/228.5kph in fourth! The first were little different from the racers save for carpets and door pockets but the later Mark III changed the right-hand gearchange for a central lever and the excellent, fixed 'hammock' seats and adjustable pedals for moveable seats. It also lost a few horsepower, and was not as popular as the earlier car, with only about half a dozen sold.

Even today, driving a GT40 is a remarkable experi-ence. The power and acceleration are truly awesome, with 0–60mph/96.5kph in around five seconds and 100mph/161kph in not much more than ten. Even with the slightly softer road suspension and on wide (but not excessively so) wire wheels, the amount of grip and precision of handling are exceptional, with so much flexible power that it is relatively easy to balance the car on the throttle through fast corners. The steering is super quick, the gearbox is slick per-fection, and the only thing that really betrays the car is the massive effort needed to get the best from the big disc brakes.

The roadgoing GT40 really is a very special legacy of 'total performance' – almost certainly the last all-out racing sportscar which could double as such a docile yet shatteringly quick road car; and it was also the Ford that beat Ferrari. At last there was an American sportscar that matched European perform-ance.

1966 LAMBORGHINI MIURA

In the 1960s, when Italian industrialist Ferruccio Lamborghini branched out into the hazardous business of building sportscars, he did so with the intention of beating Enzo Ferrari at his own game. He acted out of a frustration common to many Ferrari owners at the cavalier attitude of Ferrari towards customers who dared find fault with his cars.

Lamborghini was not a man to do things by halves. His substantial fortune was based on building tractors and air conditioning systems. For his badge he chose the bull of his birth sign – and his head-on approach matched it perfectly. He committed himself to building cars to match any Ferrari in performance but without their often unruly temperament or uncompromising ascendancy of engineering over creature comforts.

Against all the odds, he succeeded. His engineering team was young but gifted and his production standards exquisite. His first car, the 350GT, was launched in 1964, with a magnificent 3.5-litre four cam V12 designed by Giotto Bizzarrini. Bizzarrini had just left Ferrari (none too happily) after being closely involved in developing the great GTO and several other racing models. His 602 Lamborghini V12 was a logical progression of his Ferrari work, not a copy. It survives in developed form in today's Countach S.

In 1965 the engine grew to a full 4-litres for the 400GT, introduced at that year's Geneva Show. Alongside the 400GT was a rolling chassis, also with the new 4-litre V12. In this case, it was mounted transversely behind the two-seater cockpit with its five-speed gearbox and final drive cleverly integrated into a modified crankcase. Designed, like the earlier cars, by Gianpaolo Dallara, it was labelled TP400 – for *transversale posteriore* 4-litre. Most people thought it was either a one-off show car or a racing prototype.

They were wrong: Lamborghini never did fall into the financially-perilous racing trap and in 1966 the TP400 re-emerged with a lovely Bertone body as the production Miura. Until then, Lamborghini had only partly fulfilled his dream to upstage Ferrari; with the Miura he beat his rival into the mid-engined supercar league by eight full years.

Simply, he created a car combining near racing standards of performance with luxury appointments

1966 LAMBORGHINI MIURA	
Engine	V12, 4ohc
Capacity	3.9 litres
Maximum power	350bhp
Chassis/suspension	Mid-engine lightweight platform, independent coil spring/wishbone
Top speed	170mph
0–60mph	6.0 seconds

ABOVE *Combining racing car performance and limousine luxury, the Lamborghini Miura is a true Italian supercar in the Ferrari league.*

and an almost limousine comfort.

Dallara's chassis was not the usual tubular affair, but a platform with box section sills, centre and cross members. It was liberally riddled with holes for lightness but immensely strong – a prerequisite for decent road manners, whatever the suspension system. It was complicated and expensive to make, more so because of Lamborghini's insistence on making virtually everything in-house and this more than anything limited the number of Miuras made. Demand, however, always easily outstripped supply.

Not only was the Miura utterly beautiful, it was as quick as it looked. It started as the P400, with 350bhp, and grew with appropriate chassis improvements through the 370bhp P400S of 1969 to the ultimate Miura, the 1971 P400SV, with 385bhp and subtle but unmistakeable aerodynamic tweaks based on a stillborn racing design, the Jota.

In SV form, the Miura would achieve well over 170mph/273.5kph, hit 60mph/96.5kph in under six seconds and 100mph/161kph in 14 seconds. On wishbone and coil spring suspension all round, it combined a supple ride with marvellous roadholding – although it was undeniably nervous around its eventual limits, especially in the early versions, and it did have a tendency to lift its nose at very high speeds. It was also short on luggage space and the interior luxury was offset by a dozen big air intakes woofing greedily away only inches behind the occupants' heads.

The Miura was a landmark; an engineering *tour de force* which rewarded a skilled driver with staggering performance and lesser mortals with a special symbol of style. Lamborghini sold just 760 Miuras of various kinds up to 1973, shortly after which it was replaced by the even more remarkable Countach – which is still in production.

1967 FERRARI 365GTB4 DAYTONA

The identity of the all-time number one sportscar is a prolonged argument – and, of course, there is no real answer. Sportscars are such a personal thing and there are so many worthy claimants to greatness that trying to single out one is as frustrating as it would be meaningless.

Ask a hundred enthusiasts to list their own all-time top-ten in no particular order, and there is a fair chance that the Ferrari 365GTB4, the Daytona, would be on every list.

The Daytona, more than any other sportscar with the possible exception of the Cobra, has become a popular legend. It takes a real enthusiast to know the genius of Lamborghini or a Bugatti, but a Ferrari can strike a chord in almost anybody – and no Ferrari more so than the classic Daytona.

Even by Ferrari's standards, the Daytona was a milestone: the ultimate expression of the big front-engined V12 bloodline and the pinnacle of one great Ferrari tradition. It was also almost certainly the fastest genuine road car ever to prove its claims against the stopwatch, long past its own production lifetime and even now with few legitimate challengers.

Yet it was a docile and totally civilized Grand Touring car with a restrained elegance that would turn heads anywhere, but never raise eyebrows.

It was unveiled at the 1968 Paris Salon, as a logical successor to the 275GTB4. The designation 365GTB4 represented the capacity of one of its dozen cylinders, the body type *Gran Turismo Berlina* and the number of its cams – four. Later, there would be a tantalisingly small sprinkling of another Daytona, the 365GTS4 – where the S stood for *Spyder*, or open top.

The Lampredi-designed 602 V12 displaced 4390cc and delivered 352bhp at 7700rpm, with 318lb ft of torque at a fairly high 5500rpm. The torque spread, however, was prodigious and the lazy effortlessness of the power delivery gave the car a character all its own.

The beautiful alloy body, with its steeply raked windscreen and high waistline, was designed by Pininfarina and built by Scaglietti. There was no superfluous embelishment; the racing pattern cast magnesium wheels were the Daytona's only small cry for attention; even the Prancing Horse badges were tiny, but such a car could only be a Ferrari.

1967 FERRARI 365GTB DAYTONA	
Engine	V12, 4ohc
Capacity	4.4 litres
Maximum power	325bhp
Chassis/suspension	Multitubular independent coil spring/wishbone all round
Top speed	174mph
0–60mph	5.3 seconds

Under the long bonnet (hood), the heavy V12 was set well back, to produce near perfect weight distribution – helped by the five-speed gearbox and final drive being mounted in unit with the independent rear suspension. It gave the big car – 14½ft and over 1½ tons – staggering performance.

The Daytona would do an honest 174mph/280kph, but it was also perfectly friendly. Effective aerodynamic detailing made it absolutely stable, even at its maximum speed, and its handling was equally protective.

Coil spring and wishbone suspension all round (just like Ferrari's contemporary racers) offered outstanding handling potential to the skilled driver, without demanding any ability out of the ordinary (save a degree of physical strength and stamina for the generally heavy controls).

Below its considerable limits, the Daytona was no more demanding to drive than any big, gentle saloon and perhaps its greatest strength of all was, as its name implied, a real, long-legged Grand Tourer – with the emphasis on the Grand.

In 1974, this last of the front-engined V12 Ferrari line made way for the first of the mid-engined 12-cylinder Ferraris, the 365GTBB – or *Berlinetta Boxer*. The Boxer part gave away the configuration of the car's new flat-12 engine, which had the same, horizontally-opposed layout as Ferrari's contemporary Grand Prix racers. It had the same capacity as the Daytona's V12, the same torque and a little more horsepower.

The Boxer was, and in its latest 388bhp guise still is, a great car, but the Daytona was perhaps the greatest of all.

ABOVE AND LEFT *The greatest Ferrari of all? A totally civilized Grand Tourer, with bite where it counts, the Daytona will probably go down in history as the ultimate Ferrari. Whether in Berlinetta* (ABOVE) *or Spyder* (LEFT) *bodyshell the Daytona is no more difficult to drive than a big saloon car – its aero-dynamics keep it rock steady right up to the 174 mph/ 278.4 kph maximum.*

1968 MORGAN PLUS 8

While any number of small companies worldwide build replicas of classic sportscars from long-gone eras, the Morgan company goes one stage better: it builds *real* sportscars from a long-gone era. That, at least, is the way it seems, but in spite of a basic shape, unchanged since the first four-wheeler Morgan appeared in 1936, and a suspension layout shared with the very first Morgan of 1910, the Morgan Plus 8 successfully combines classic character with modern performance in a way that no one else even approaches.

The Plus 8, launched in 1968 and still going strong, says it all about the Morgan philosophy.

It was introduced because Morgan needed something a bit special to revive its image after the end of its Triumph TR powered Plus 4 series. Having failed miserably to interest buyers in the modern shape of the fibre-glass-bodied Plus 4 Plus coupé, Morgan rightly resigned themselves to the fact that people still wanted a traditional Morgan. This, however, could still be spectacular.

After complex negotiations (and rejection of several alternatives) Morgan arranged to use Rover's recently adopted 3.5-litre development of the small block, all-alloy Buick V8 for its new flagship. By February 1967 they had built a Plus 4 based prototype and by the end of the year the idea was almost ready for production.

In the end, the Plus 8 chassis was slightly longer and wider at the front (dispensing with the unsightly bonnet (hood) bulges of the prototype), and had its rear springs shifted back to ease the axle tramp generated by the V8's power. The whole development programme supposedly cost Morgan about today's price of a single car!

It was an excellent investment; 18 years after the model was introduced, Morgan still has probably the longest waiting list of any car company in the world. Order a new Plus 8 now and you might drive it away in about five years time.

If you did you would find a car of exceptional character and electrifying performance — at least until high-speed aerodynamics take over.

The Plus 8 has changed very little since its introduction. The Z-section ladder chassis still has the famous sliding-pillar and coil spring front suspension, plus a solid axle on semi-elliptic springs at the

ABOVE *Using traditional craftsmanship for the body (hand-beaten aluminium on an ash frame), and allying it to the light-alloy Rover V8, the Malvern-built Morgan Plus 8 is a true sportscar for the 1980s.*

1968 MORGAN PLUS 8	
Engine	Rover V8, ohv
Capacity	3.5 litres
Maximum power	151bhp
Chassis/suspension	Ladder chassis, coil spring/sliding pillar ifs, semi-elliptic rear
Top speed	123mph
0–60mph	6.5 seconds

rear – with lever dampers to complete the 'vintage' specification.

Early cars had a Moss four-speed close-ratio gearbox, remote from the engine. This unit, whose excellent ratios were offset by a very difficult change, was replaced by a four-speed Rover 'box (in unit with the engine) in 1972. At the same time, the car grew a touch wider in track and acquired slightly bigger tyres, with minor bodywork changes to suit. In 1975 an alloy-panelled lightweight version was offered (built, like the steel-bodied car) over a traditional wood frame, but few were sold.

The car was very light anyway, at only 17cwt, helped by the all-alloy engine and the light Rover gearbox. It shed a few more pounds in 1977 when it adopted the latest Rover five-speed gearbox and the 155bhp version of the V8 that went with it. Power output had already varied slightly, from the originally quoted 160bhp, through 151bhp and 143bhp (on a lower compression ratio from 1973). There were other minor changes, notably to wheels and tyres, which standardized 15-inch rims with Pirelli P6 covers early in 1982, and to the steering, with rack-and-pinion as a welcome option from 1983 and, subsequently, a less 'nervous' recirculating ball system as standard.

The biggest change, as an option, came in 1984, when Morgan offered the fuel-injected 190bhp Rover Vitesse engine, to give the Plus 8 even more staggering performance. Where the 155bhp car is good for some 123mph and 0-60 times of 6.5 seconds, the injected Moggie will nudge 130mph and carve the 60mph sprint down to just six seconds.

With a very open-air driving position, a harsh ride on all but the smoothest roads (but superb roadholding and brakes) and a generally 'alive' character, it feels even quicker. Anachronism it may be, but it is fantastic fun.

LEFT *Visually, the Morgan has hardly changed since the 1930s. Driver comfort hasn't changed much either, with a bone-jarring ride over even the smallest bumps – real seat-of-the-pants motoring.*

1969 NISSAN 240Z

It was only a matter of time before the Japanese solved the problem of breaking into the sportscar market. When Nissan did it they did so in the biggest possible way, their 240Z quickly becoming the biggest selling sportscar in the world.

As elsewhere, Japanese ascendancy in the motor industry was based more on making other people's ideas work better than on inventing anything new. Nissan had produced previous sportscars, but anything before the 240Z had only sold in tiny numbers to a specialized market. To Western eyes, most of what went before was idiosyncratic; European and American sportscar buyers brought up on the old-fashioned simplicity of MGs, Austin-Healeys, Triumphs and the like were too ready to mistake clever engineering for unproven novelty.

Japan did make mistakes, but that was not one of them. Their biggest error was, that in spite of their worldwide success, their cars were still peculiarly Japanese – and in particular, most were built to suit the smaller Japanese physique. In saloon cars this was not so obvious, but in first generation Japanese sportscars (of which the Honda S800 was a fair example) big drivers had problems.

Fortunately for Nissan, the man who helped initiate the 240Z programme, as a successor to the MGB-like Fairlady SR3, stylist Albrecht Goertz, was a German, based in New York. He insisted that his car be designed around Western rather than Eastern physiques, even if that made it a pure two-seater rather than the planned 2+2.

His outline design drew on American, Germany and British styling ideas. In 1964 it was translated into a prototype for Nissan by Yamaha, who also built the 2-litre six-cylinder twin-cam engine, but Nissan dropped the whole project after numerous technical problems arose. It was revived in 1966 by Nissan's own engineers, with the more conventional intention of building a car around available running gear – in this case a 151bhp 2.4-litre straight-six engine based on the four-cylinder Bluebird saloon car unit.

It had a unit-construction two-door shell, designed for mass production, with MacPherson strut suspension all round. Brakes were discs at the front, finned drums at the rear, and steering was by rack-and-pinion. A four-speed gearbox was standard for the

USA and the superb, close-ratio five-speed which was optional there was standard elsewhere.

As launched in November 1969, the 240Z was not revolutionary, just a well-honed example of existing technology. A 2-litre version, the Fairlady Z was sold in Japan, but the 240Z's biggest market was the USA, where it was soon labelled as being in a class of its own for its very low price – way ahead of obvious rivals like the MGB and Triumph GT6 in every respect, and much closer to the more expensive E-Type or Porsche.

The 240Z was spiritual successor to the macho European sportscar typified by the 'Big Healeys' – which burgeoning US legislation killed in 1968. It was ready for the rules which killed the Healey.

Most significantly, the Nissan 240Z was always a coupé, never a soft-top, which also let Nissan equip it to the interior standards which Japan considered normal. It was well trimmed, though the seats were none too comfortable, it had a full range of instruments and even a radio. Air conditioning was optional on US-bound cars.

On the road, the flexible, silky smooth engine gave 125mph/265.5kph performance with 0-60mph/96.5kph in under eight seconds and comfortable 120mph/193kph cruising. The handling was crisp and near neutral, with power oversteer on tap and very responsive steering.

Sales boomed and Nissan soon doubled its planned production rate but still took almost three years to catch up with demand.

In 1973 the 240Z was replaced by the 260Z, whose bigger engine did not make up for more de-toxing and more weight. Later Z cars grew bigger and softer and although the current 300ZX Turbo has a style of its own, the 240Z remains the best of all.

1969 DATSUN 240Z	
Engine	In-line, 6-cyl, sohc
Capacity	2.4 litres
Maximum power	151bhp
Chassis/suspension	Unitary construction, MacPherson strut, iars
Top speed	125mph
0–60mph	7.8 seconds

LEFT *Generally regarded as the best of the Nissan 'Z-cars' the 240Z was the first in a long line of Japanese sportscars. With performance to take on E-Types and Porsches, the 240Z proved successful both on the road and in competition.*

1971 DE TOMASO PANTERA

Attractive though the idea is, very few manufacturers have made a success of substituting big, cheap American V8 power with the prohibitively expensive alternative of manufacturing engines from scratch. Even fewer have made the logical progression that the De Tomaso Pantera made in 1970, to the mid-engined format, even though the V8 is an obvious choice for such treatment.

After all, in the mid-1960s and early 1970s big American V8 mid-engines proliferated in European as well as American motor racing – in both Can-Am type sportscars and Formula 5000/Formula A single seaters, Ford, with the Le Mans winning GT40 – the spiritual ancestor of all roadgoing mid-engined supercars – had showed that the idea *could* work on the road, yet most of the big V8 users stuck conservatively with the old front-engined layout.

Surprisingly, as both the basic parameters and most of the hardware were readily and fairly cheaply available from the racing world, no more than one or two tried to follow Ford's lead; they simply left mid-engines to the real supercar builders. Of the handful who tried, the De Tomaso Pantera was the only long-term success.

The Argentine former racing driver, Allejandro de Tomaso, had built some reasonably successful cars before the Pantera, but this soon overshadowed them all. His first mid-engined car was the smaller Vallelunga and in 1966 he launched the evil-handling 4.7-litre V8 Mangusta.

In 1967 he bought Ghia, the firm which styled the Mangusta. When Ford subsequently took over Ghia, Tomaso found an unlikely but enthusiastic ally. The giant US manufacturer saw in the underdeveloped Mangusta the possibility of something better. With its glamorous Italian name and Ford power, its racy

1971 DE TOMASO PANTERA	
Engine	Ford V8, ohv
Capacity	5.7 litres
Maximum power	330bhp
Chassis/suspension	Mid-engine, unitary, coil spring/wishbone iars
Top speed	160mph
0–60mph	5.6 seconds

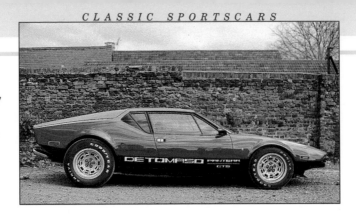

BELOW AND RIGHT *The De Tomaso Pantera GTS, styled by Ghia and powered by Ford. Good looks and handling, and a mid-mounted engine make it a car to be reckoned with.*

image might pull buyers into Ford showrooms and closer to more mundane products without Ford having to commit itself to an expensive full-scale sportscar programme.

So, with Ford's help, the mid-engined basics were considerably refined, given an attractive new body evolved by Ghia in Ford's Detroit wind tunnels, and re-launched at the 1970 New York Motor Show as the De Tomaso Pantera, 'Powered by Ford'.

With the weight of Ford backing, and access to many corporate parts bins, it had become a very civilized car. The 5.7-litre V8 and a five-speed ZF transaxle were mounted in a subframe in the back of a steel, unit-construction two-seater coupé shell. It stood on coil spring and wishbone suspension, with ventilated disc brakes all round, and rather larger tyres on the back than on the front – which not only gave it the sportly looks that Ford wanted but also reduced the handling effects of the considerable rearward weight bias.

It was quite a big car, at almost exactly 14ft long. With its robust build and high equipment levels (even air conditioning was offered) it was also heavier than it should have been, not much short of a ton-and-a-half. The standard engine in the L version gave 330bhp at 5,400rpm and 325lb ft of torque at only 3,500rpm, enough for spectacular acceleration to a top speed of around 160mph/257kph.

Within a year, Ford had approved a limited endurance racing programme for the Pantera but the car

1972 FIAT X1/9

When Fiat introduced the X1/9, in November 1972, they were not by any means the first to explore the mid-engined format for sportscars. By the mid-1960s the layout was essential for racing and by 1972 Ferrari (with the Dino), Lotus, Porsche (with the unloved 914), Lamborghini and Maserati could all offer mid-engined road cars. What Fiat achieved, where even Porsche had failed, was to put the concept into actual mass production, selling large numbers of a sophisticated idea to a market hitherto happy with cheap and cheerful sportscar engineering from the likes of MG, Triumph, Alfa Romeo — even Fiat themselves.

At first, Fiat were as reticent about such a radical change as the surprisingly conservative buyers were. They were talked into the X1/9 project by Bertone, who had come up with the germ of the idea in a typically extravagant but quite workable show-car concept. Their two-seater Runabout appeared at the Turin Show in November 1969, with a 903cc Fiat engine. Apart from silly headlights mounted on its Targa-style roof bar, it is recognisably the basis of the X1/9.

Bertone were struggling to fit a sportscar into the new front-wheel-drive Fiat 128 family. They badly needed to style a replacement for the rear-engined 850 Spyder, but until Nuccio Bertone moved the front-wheel-drive power pack to the other end of the car they were not even come close to solving the problem of the 850's 128-based successor.

Soon after the Turin Show, Bertone built a running 128-based prototype. When Fiat eventually accepted it, the X1/9's long gestation began.

Revealed as a production model in November 1972, it was a two-seater, with limited luggage space in the nose and in a compartment behind the transverse mid-engine. It had a distinctive wedge shape and a removable Targa top which stowed in the front luggage space. The fuel tank was behind the bulkhead aft of one seat and the spare wheel was behind the other. It was a masterpiece of packaging both in cramming so much into so small a space and in keeping the major masses within the wheelbase, contributing to fantastic roadholding.

It used a mildly modified 128 engine, fitted more upright than in the saloons for better access. In single carburettor form the 1290cc overhead-cam four-

1972 FIAT X1/9	
Engine	In-line, 4-cyl, sohc
Capacity	1.3 litres
Maximum power	75bhp
Chassis/suspension	Mid-engine, unitary, independent MacPherson strut all round
Top speed	100mph
0–60mph	12.8 seconds

cylinder unit gave 75bhp at 6000rpm and 72lb ft of torque at 3400rpm – but only a meagre 66bhp and 68lb ft when strangled by US emission regulations.

Nevertheless, when it went on sale in the USA in 1974 (having been launched in Italy in mid-1973) it became a major success. The key was its remarkable handling and roadholding and its sheer style. Its trim was basic, tinny even in places; like the small MGs and Triumphs, its power train was borrowed from a saloon, but at its price nothing approached its style or leech-like grip.

It only offered between 93 and 100mph depending on market, but on 128-based MacPherson strut suspension it gave almost neutral, almost idiot-proof handling, instant steering response, and cornering power way beyond the reach of its mass-produced rivals. Even with 0-60 times of almost 13 seconds, it was often labelled 'a mini Ferrari'.

Fiat were in no hurry to change it. In 1976 it grew bigger bumpers for the USA. A right-hand-drive X1/9 was added in 1977; the British model offered better trim and equipment, including alloy wheels and even a fitted luggage set.

In October 1978 the new Ritmo's 1498cc engine answered criticism that the brilliant chassis deserved more power. The X1/9 1500 had 85bhp; with much better torque and a five-speed gearbox it had far more flexible performance and up to 110mph. US cars had only 65bhp and were heavier – but from 1980 a fuel-injection option (standard after 1982) gave 75bhp – just like the original European 1300!

It wasn't lack of power that eventually hurt the X1/9 most; Fiat's widespread quality control problems of the early 1980s brought a near fatal slump in sales and transfer of much reduced production to Bertone in 1981, since when the car has survived only as a low volume model.

LEFT *Another sleek creation from the Bertone styling studio, that made it through into mass-production is the Fiat X1/9.*

ABOVE LEFT *The distinctive wedgeshape of the X1/9 succeeds where so many other car designs in the same vein failed.*

1972 LANCIA STRATOS

Once the Lancia Stratos had been built, its years of near invincibility in rallying were assured, but it was a minor miracle that the Stratos was built at all. Only two years before the first prototype was shown, at the Turin Show late in 1971, Lancia was all but bankrupt. Had Fiat not taken over the company in October 1969, its long and distinguished history might have ended before the 1970s. Yet without the financial problems and consequent Fiat connection the Stratos would not have happened anyway.

1972 LANCIA STRATOS	
Engine	Ferrari Dino V6, 4ohc
Capacity	2.4 litres
Maximum power	190bhp
Chassis/suspension	Mid-engine monocoque centre with extensions, coil spring ifs
Top speed	142mph
0–60mph	6.6 seconds

ABOVE *The road-going version of the mid-engined Lancia Stratos which dominated the world rally scene for years.*

was too big and thirsty to mix it with the contemporary Porsches and Ferraris.

That increased Ford's disillusionment with the Pantera, which actually sold quite well but never really made people think of Ford. With the early 1970s oil crisis and the growing consumer lobby, performance was no longer a very good word to sell. Quietly, by 1974, Ford eased out of its direct involvement with the Pantera, although it continued to use Ford engines. The GTS version boasted wider wheels, more radical bodywork and up to 350bhp. The even more spectacular GTS 'Silhouette' evoked the racing image with matt black trim, huge wheels and arch extensions, a deep, wrap-around nose spoiler and a massive rear wing (fender) – plus enough power to make it almost as quick as it looked.

Under all the glitter, it sold in fairly large numbers, but without the Ford connection it was only a fringe model. When de Tomaso took over Maserati in 1976 he might have dropped the Pantera, but it has survived – and after weathering a major sales slump is still unique in its stock-block mid-engined format.

Another of Fiat's commercial acquisitions was the catalyst for the forerunner of today's rally supercars. In June 1969, shortly before the Lancia takeover, Fiat had acquired a half-share in Ferrari. Fiat extended Ferrari's manufacturing scope (and homologation possibilities) by building the 2.4-litre Dino V6 engine, supplying some of the Ferrari-built mid-engined Dino and fitting many more into their own front-engined Fiat Dino.

After the Fiat takeover, Lancia had a real future, with generous investment in new models and enough backing for a proper rally programme. The front-wheel-drive Fulvia was a prolific winner, and world champion, but by the early 1970s Lancia could see the growing threat from rear- and mid-engined cars like the Alpine-Renault, Porsche 911 and the ultimately abortive Ford GT70.

Lancia competition chief Cesare Fiorio knew a mid-engined car with the solution; in the Ferrari V6 he saw the ideal basis for his car. Thanks to the Fiat connection, the deal was possible (if not universally popular) so all Fiorio needed was a car.

He already had its name and basic inspiration, from a futuristic, Lancia-engined Bertone showcar, seen at Turin in 1970: the Stratos.

The real thing shared only the name, wheelbase and the maker, as Bertone were entrusted with designing not only the body but also the chassis of the new rally car – and then making the 500 units necessary to qualify it for competition. Lancia would complete the final assembly.

Bertone's chassis (their first ever!) used a steel monocoque centre section with sheet, box and tubular extensions at the front and a massively strong rear cage for the transversely-mounted mid-engine, transmission and suspension.

Around this stubby base they built a stunning fibreglass shell. It looked almost as wide as it was long, was exaggeratedly wedge-shaped, and the rake of its beautifully curved screen, swept by one huge wiper, followed the slope of the heavily-louvred nose. The first cars had no superfluous trim; the distinctive (and effective) roof and tail spoilers were only added to later cars. The leather straps on the hinged nose and tail sections (vital for mechanical accessibility) were there to keep the lightweight panels in line with the rest of the car.

In every respect, the Stratos was an unqualified success. From the start it was a rally and race winner and its eventual tally included four Monte Carlo Rallies and a hat-trick of world championships. Its career might have been even longer except that by 1978, marketing needs put the Fiat name to the fore, with the Abarth 131.

ABOVE *Power comes from the Ferrari Dino engine sitting behind the driver.*

RIGHT *The glassfibre body of the Stratos was styled and built by Bertone.*

1972 MASERATI BORA

ABOVE *The Maserati Bora, like many supercars of its day, is mid-engined and developed from Maserati's racing expertise. Its main drawback is the Citroën-derived braking system which has little 'feel'.*

Like Ferrari, Maserati started out reluctantly as a road car manufacturer, and like Ferrari only really went into production at all as a way of paying for its primary interest, motor racing.

Enzo Ferrari had a long career in racing, as a driver and a manager (with Alfa Romeo), before he became a manufacturer in his own right immediately before World War II. When he started building Ferraris after the war, he quickly, if a little cynically, cashed in on roadgoing cars as a source of income. It took Maserati a little longer.

Maserati was a racing car manufacturer (a highly successful one) from 1926. Some of their racing sportscars were usable on the road but that was incidental. The first Maserati intended for the road appeared in 1950, after the Maserati brothers had sold the business to the wealthy industrialist and racing enthusiast, Omer Orsi.

The two-door A6 coupé of 1950 was introduced not out of choice but of necessity, to help offset mounting losses for the racing time. It took Maserati another seven years to get serious about road car production – still basically for racing finance – with the lovely, six-cylinder, twin-cam 3,500, built with various body styles until 1964.

Thereafter, Maserati built quite a mixture of road cars, many of them excellent, but somehow never seeming to generate the charisma of a Ferrari or a Lamborghini.

In many people's eyes, the best Maserati of all came at a time when the company was going through an even deeper crisis than usual. It was the V8-engined Bora, introduced at the Geneva Show in March 1971, widely acclaimed but often overlooked in the super-car stakes, although it stayed in production, against the odds, until 1980.

Like other new generation supercars, it was mid-engined, in this case with a truly excellent V8 of Maserati's own making and developed from their successful 4.5-litre sports racing cars of the mid-to-late 1960s.

It was a light, compact, all-alloy unit with twin overhead cams and fed by four twin-choke down-draught Weber carbs. It started life at 4.7-litres, which gave 310bhp at 6,000rpm, and an even more impressive 340lb ft of torque. It grew later to just over 4.9-litres, adding another 20bhp and becoming even

1972 MASERATI BORA	
Engine	V8, 4ohc
Capacity	4.7 litres
Maximum power	310bhp
Chassis/suspension	Mid-engine, unitary, coil spring/ wishbone iars
Top speed	157mph
0–60mph	6.2 seconds

more willing at low revs – helped by five perfectly chosen gear ratios in a 'box mounted, racing style, behind the final drive.

All this sat in a tubular subframe at the back of a steel unit-construction two-door coupé shell, by master-stylist Giugiaro. It was properly equipped, even to the extent of standard air conditioning, electric windows and automatically adjustable seats and pedals.

The Bora was quite capable of exploiting all its near-160mph/257kph performance. On coil spring and wishbone suspension it had near perfect hand-ling balance and exceptional grip even by these standards – although exploiting the higher reaches demanded a degree of skill and a slice of bravery.

If it had a fault it was in the braking system. In 1968 Citroën had taken over Maserati during one of its periodic crises. Citroën gained a Maserati-developed V6 for its SM saloon (also used in a slightly modified Bora shell as the supposedly 2+2 Merak) and Maserati gained Citroën's electro-hydraulic braking system. This was hardly a fair swap; the Bora's disc brakes were fine, but the button on the floor where the pedal should be was a strictly on-off affair with no feel and no place in an otherwise great car.

If the Bora had not been as good as it was, it might only have survived a couple of years. In 1973 the Citroën association ended and during the oil crisis of that time the company all but folded. Production actually stopped until 1976, by which time Maserati had been taken over by Allejandro de Tomaso – a man with a powerful survival instinct. The Bora continued until 1980; de Tomaso has lasted a little longer and with his help the greatest days of all for Maserati's road cars might still be to come.

1974 LAMBORGHINI COUNTACH

Ferrucio Lamborghini had a way with words; no name could have been more appropriate for his first V12 mid-engined supercar than Miura – the name of a particularly brave and pure-bred fighting bull. For a while though, Lamborghini was at a loss for a suitable name for the Miura's even more sensational V12-engined successor.

According to legend, local workers solved the problem for him the first time the prototype of the new car was wheeled out in public. They took one look at the sleek, futuristic, swing-up door device and exclaimed, simply: *Countach*! This is a word from the expressive local Piedmontese dialect and the nearest printable translation is something to the effect of 'Wow!'.

So, Countach the new car was.

Although it uses essentially the same V12 engine as the Miura, it is a very different car indeed. Without any argument, it is quite the most spectacular-looking production car in the world. More than 15 years after the LP500 prototype was unveiled on the Bertone stand at the Geneva Show in 1971, the Countach *still* looks futuristic! Over the years it has grown even more dramatic with the gradual addition of aerodynamic aids and more massive modern rubber on the road to deal with increased horsepower.

The original designation, LP, states the biggest change from the Miura, which first appeared as the TP400. Both cars were mid-engined, but where the Miura's TP mean *transversale posteriore* (rear, transverse), the Countach's LP means *longitudinale posteriore* (rear, in line). The difference did not simply amount to turning the big alloy engine through 90°. The Miura had a clever gearbox and final drive built into its crankcase; the Countach uses a more conventional arrangement with its five-speed gearbox on the forward end of the block, bringing the gearbox between the occupants and the gearlever to the driver's hand with no additional linkage. Less conventionally, drive is fed back by a shaft running through the sump, to a final drive at the back of the engine.

The Countach did not go into proper production, as the LP400, until 1974, by which time it had undergone several changes from the prototype. The engine had returned from 5-litres to the Miura's 4-litres, and 375bhp at 8,000rpm; the planned monocoque chassis

RIGHT *Little more than a thinly-disguised racing car, the Lamborghini Countach offers stunning performance. The sleek alloy bodyshell hides a tubular spaceframe chassis. Rear visibility is negligible through the tiny rear screen – but you would probably be looking ahead anyway at 170 mph/272 kph!*

gave way to a fantastically complex and highly effective multi-tubular spaceframe, with welded-on alloy panels. Also, the originally uncluttered shape sprouted its first tweaks, with both NACA ducts and airboxes by the rear quarters for cooling – which had proved to be a major problem area. It retained the dramatic door opening arrangement by which the doors swung up and forward in an arc around their top leading corner, counterbalanced by hydraulic struts.

The fully adjustable suspension was by coil springs and wishbones at the front, and coil springs, wishbones, top and trailing links at the back. The brakes too, were virtually to racing specifications, with large ventilated discs and four-pot calipers. Like the rest of the car, they were well up to the expected performance.

The Countach was shatteringly fast (though not as fast as the maker's claims of 190mph/306kph) and at over 170mph/273.5kph its handling and roadholding were everything that even the most demanding driver could hope for. It had firm suspension with almost no body roll and, now that it has tyres to match the chassis ability, has grip racing standard.

Changes began in 1978 with the much better shod Countach 400S, which also had considerably wider wheel arches to suit, plus the option of a large rear aerofoil – announcing the Countach's even more aggressive look. The next change came in 1982 with the Countach LP500S, which in spite of its designation originally had a 4.8-litre version of the V12, with a claimed 400bhp. Finally the Countach has gained four-valve cylinder heads which puts it firmly back among the latest generation of Ferraris and Porsches for performance.

Common to this class of car, the Countach could, of course, offer more in the way of comfort, petrol consumption and noise level. This, however, can be overlooked in favour of its stunning performance.

1986 LAMBORGHINI COUNTACH QUATTROVALVOLE	
Engine	V12, 4ohc, 48v
Capacity	5.2 litres
Maximum power	455bhp
Chassis/suspension	Multitubular spaceframe, coil spring iars
Top speed	190mph
0–60mph	4.5 seconds

1975 PORSCHE 911 TURBO

Looking at today's Porsche 911 Turbo, lean, mean and purposeful with wide wheels, sweeping arches and huge picnic-table wing, it is hard to remember that the basic 911 shape is over 20 years old, first seen in September 1964. In fact, the 911 was only Porsche's second series since the company had become a manufacturer in its own right in 1950 – and its resemblance to that first series is quite recognizable, even now.

Part of what has helped the 911 survive for so long and still look so fresh is the functional simplicity of its styling – drawn initially by Ferry Porsche, son of the company founder, Dr Ferdinand Porsche.

The 911 followed the mechanical layout of the 356 which it replaced. It was a rear-engined 2+2 coupé, and its engine was air-cooled and horizontally opposed. The first 356 engines had been modified versions of the humble flat-four Volkswagen Beetle engine (reasonable enough, because Dr Porsche had designed that car too), but the 911 was introduced with a Porsche 2-litre flat-six, producing 130bhp.

The other part of the 911 survival formula has been the steady increase in power over the years, through capacity increases and then turbocharging – all backed by continual chassis and aerodynamic development, but without ever changing the basics. In 1970 the 911 grew to 2.2-litres and offered fuel injection as an option to the standard carburettors; by 1972 it was up to 2.3-litres and then late in 1973 went up to 2.7-litres, with injection as standard. What seemed at the time to be the ultimate 911 was launched in 1973: the lightweight, more highly-tuned Carrera RS series.

Quick though the RS was, at up to 150mph/241kph, Porsche had more to come, and in 1975 they introduced the first 3-litre, 260bhp Turbo, officially type-numbered the 930, badged simply Turbo, but generally known as the 911 Turbo.

It developed into successful racing models, the 934 and 935 (which dominated endurance racing for many years, in numbers and results) and became more popular as a road car than anyone had dreamed. Even after Porsche launched its V8 front-engined 928 series, the 911 types dominated the company's supercar sales and still show no signs of losing their magic in the foreseeable future.

In 1977 the Turbo grew again, to a full 3.3-litres,

RIGHT With most of its weight at the rear, the Porsche 911 Turbo shouldn't handle at all, yet it will hold its own with any of the latest generation of mid-engine sports coupés. With its turbocharged, flat-six, 3.3-litre engine howling away at the back, the 911 Turbo passes 60 mph in just over five seconds – not bad for a design that's basically over 20 years old.

1986 PORSCHE TURBO	
Engine	A/c, flat 6-cyl, turbo
Capacity	3.3 litres
Maximum power	300bhp
Chassis/suspension	Rear-engined, platform chassis, MacPherson strut ifs, torsion bars
Top speed	160mph
0–60mph	5.2 seconds

staying there ever since and keeping the car firmly among the fastest in the world. Power is up to 300bhp at 5500rpm, with tremendous torque at all speeds. Most important, the extra capacity and general development all but eliminated the characteristic throttle lag which early Turbos suffered. The engine is now virtually as responsive as any free-breathing type.

The power is not squandered on excess weight; the compact 911 is typically Porsche in that everything, absolutely everything, is doing something – almost to racing standards, but with comfort built in. The aerodynamics are exceptional and the big rear spoiler (which houses the turbo intercooler) is totally functional. It helps give arrow-like stability at the huge speeds which the Porsche is capable of almost anywhere. Top speed is about 160mph/275kph and no other car in the world combines the Turbo's acceleration (with 0-60mph/96.5kph in about five seconds dead) with such dramatic, instant responsiveness. Moreover, the Porsche has no hint of supercar temperament; it is as frugal on fuel as many cars with half its performance, and its quality and reliability are legendary.

Critics have said a car with the engine behind the back axle *must* have handling vices. The Porsche's only vice is that it will not forgive fools. Up to limits way beyond those of almost any other road car, the 911 is in a class of its own. The weight of the tail is noticeable but the grip is so formidable and the balance so perfect that the car is all but uncatchable by anything else. Only by deliberate abuse or incompetence is it possible to provoke real problems.

Maybe it is frustration that has prompted others to call the Porsche 'a triumph of development over design'. Really it is just a triumph.

LEFT AND ABOVE *The huge rear spoiler helps to keep the massive rear tyres firmly on the road and contributes to the car's high-speed stability. On the Turbo model the spoiler houses the turbocharger's intercooler.*

1977 ASTON MARTIN VANTAGE

Walk around the outside of an Aston Martin Vantage and you may be struck first by the sheer size of the car; at over 15ft long and more than six feet wide, it is big by any standards, and it weights the best part of two tons. Its size is matched by an undeniable elegance, a timeless elegance that makes it a difficult car to date, a solid, muscular elegance that is more than skin deep.

It seems crouched, ready to pounce. The deep front air-dam, below a blanked-off radiator grille, almost touches the ground; the huge bulge of the bonnet could only hide something horribly potent. It sits low, wide and square on massive sculpted wheels and squat, low-profile tyres.

Look closer and you will see a purity of line and excellence of fit that could only be achieved by traditional hand craftsmanship; you can literally see the depth of the paint – dozens of coats, hand-buffed to a finish as lustrous as Chinese lacquer and as perfect as any Rolls-Royce.

Open one of the heavy doors and everything inside is utter luxury. There are acres of deep, wool-pile carpet, edged in leather. The sumptuous 2+2 seats – far more limousine than sportscar – are leather too, and so is virtually all the other interior body trim. Over the door cappings and the dash is beautiful burr walnut, but overriding the luxury is the same air of purpose. The steering wheel and gear lever are small and chunky, a fly-off handbrake is down by the driver's seat. The instruments are classically plain, comprehensive and placed exactly right. It is a driver's car.

Under the bonnet, four cam covers and a giant air-box top an all-alloy V8 which almost fills the substantial space available. On one cover is a small brass plate bearing the name of the one man at the factory who assembled this particular engine.

For many years, while Aston Martin told his name, they omitted to tell how much power his handiwork had wrought, preferring, like Rolls-Royce, to call it 'adequate'. Now we know that the 5.4-litre engine as used in its standard form in the basic V8 saloon (latterly with Weber-Marelli fuel injection) gives a quoted 305bhp, but as modified for this sybaritic hot-rod Vantage it thumps out no less than 375bhp, with enormous torque all across the rev range.

Fed surely onto the road through an appropriately robust manual gearbox, limited-slip diff and those wide tyres, it hurls the big car forward with a blood-curdling howl of sound but less apparent fury than a stopwatch would suggest.

In reality, its size, luxury and apparently advancing years apart, the Vantage remains one of the fastest cars in the world. In the right circumstances, not necessarily wide open spaces, it will thunder up to 170mph/273kph and in spite of its huge bulk will reach 60mph/96.5kph in just five seconds – with the acceleration, incredibly, growing even more vigorous as car and engine get into their stride.

It is not just dragstrip performance either; the engine is wonderfully responsive, with no hint of temperament – just that sleeping giant power. Its chassis, though designed in the 1960s and unashamedly built for comfort, is as good as any Italian exotic. The steering is heavy in spite of power assistance, but supremely accurate and informative. The ride is firm, almost harsh, and the tyres are noisy and nervous over bad surfaces, but almost impossible to unstick at any speed in any corner except deliberately. The Vantage forgives any indiscretion save the truly unforgiveable – just as an impeccably bred English gentleman should. Even in stopping its two-ton bulk from the wrong side of 150mph/241kph it makes no fuss at all; it does that, as everything else, with an ease so understated as to be almost contemptuous.

If you need to ask how much it costs, or how far it goes on a gallon, you can't afford it. In the end, there is only one word to sum up what this fabulous motorcar has; style.

ABOVE *The interior of the Aston Martin Vantage exudes class.*
RIGHT *The timeless grace of the* Vantage *makes it look as fresh now as it was when first produced in 1977.*

1985 ASTON MARTIN VANTAGE	
Engine	V8, 4ohc
Capacity	5.4 litres
Maximum power	375bhp
Chassis/suspension	Platform chassis, coil spring independent all round
Top speed	170mph
0–60mph	5.0 seconds

1978 BMW M1 COUPÉ

A fter World War II, BMW, a company whose pre-war reputation revolved primarily around its sporting excellence, was crippled. The majority of its assets were irretrievably stuck on the wrong side of what Winston Churchill was about to dub the 'Iron Curtain'. The best of the pre-war designs had been doled out piecemeal as war reparations to the Allies – with Bristol in England taking the lion's share as the basis of its own new marque.

BMW was reduced to building what the parlous German domestic market needed most: cheap, basic, economy cars, reduced finally to the lowest denominator, a tiny bubblecar built under licence from Iso in Italy. Almost all that BMW had left after the war was a tradition and spirit.

Not until the late 1950s could the company again translate these qualities into something more tangible, with its first small sporting saloons of the post-war period.

BELOW *The M1 was developed to help BMW enter into racing, but changes in the racing regulations made it obsolete. The M1 is a superb road car – even with only 277 bhp as opposed to the 500 bhp the racing versions would have used, the car can still top 160 mph/256 kph on unrestricted roads.*

ABOVE RIGHT *The racing pedigree of the M1 shows through on the road. Softer spring to improve the ride comfort do nothing to upset the car's natural poise and stability.*

By the mid-1960s, with the coming of the 2,000 series cars, and the later coupés, BMW's image was painstakingly rehabilitated, and amply shown off by its prolific racing successes, in every category from saloon cars to Formula Two – and even, finally, in winning the Grand Prix World Championship with the Brabham team.

The only thing BMW still lacked was a front-line sports racing car which, like Ford's GT40, might sell in limited numbers as a roadgoing flagship.

In 1972, BMW unveiled a remarkable, gull-winged, mid-engined coupé, the BMW Turbo, on the show circuit. It was never intended for production, but in 1978 a car with most of the Turbo's style and character *was* unveiled as a production reality.

It was called, simply, the M1 – the M-Style logo being BMW's way of saying 'Motorsport'.

Strangely, the car had been developed to BMW's ideas by Lamborghini, who were to build it in the sort of numbers that were perfectly reasonable for them but much too small for BMW itself.

The car, powered by BMW's potent 24-valve, 3.5-litre twin-cam straight-six motor, was less radical and more practical than the show-going Turbo coupé. It had conventional doors and striking, but not excessive styling by the ubiquitous Giugiaro.

It was openly admitted that it was intended first as a racing car (with production limited to numbers appropriate to homologation requirements) but the production run was to include road cars, fully trimmed and well equipped.

Even before the M1 was announced, however, Lamborghini's own near-terminal commercial problems ended their involvement, and the car was eventually built in Germany. Unfortunately, by the time the M1 was in production, changes to international racing regulations had rendered it obsolete. It did race against open opposition, with only limited success, but BMW contrived some far more conspicuous racing exposure for their potential lemon, in the guise of the Procar series. In 1979 and 1980, racing M1s provided a supporting event at selected Grand Prix races. Alongside healthy numbers of private entries, BMW entered six works cars for the fastest Grand Prix qualifiers – a brilliant publicity exercise and a great spectacle with these 200mph/322kph supercars, but doomed to failure by the convoluted politics of driver contracts.

So, the majority of the 450 or so M1s built between 1978 and 1980 made outstanding road cars. Where racing engines could boast 500bhp (as much as 850bhp with turbocharging), the fuel injected production engine gave a perfectly adequate 277bhp and comfortable 160mph/257kph performance.

Even on softer springing and road tyres, the M1 retained much of its racing poise. Its handling combined inherent understeer with easily power-induced neutrality, or even oversteer – progressing to a more naturally tail-out stance at much higher speeds.

If bureaucracy had rendered the M1 something of a failure in its intended racing guise, nothing has taken away its brilliance as a road car and a perfect symbol of BMW's triumphant return.

1978 BMW M1 COUPÉ	
Engine	In-line, 6-cyl, sohc, 24v
Capacity	3.5 litres
Maximum power	277bhp
Chassis/suspension	Mid-engined, space frame, coil spring/wishbone iars
Top speed	160mph
0–60mph	5.8 seconds

1981 DE LOREAN GULLWING COUPÉ DMC-12

1981 DE LOREAN DMC-12	
Engine	P-R-V V6, sohc
Capacity	2.8 litres
Maximum power	156bhp
Chassis/suspension	Rear-engine, backbone, coil spring independent all round
Top speed	135mph
0–60mph	8.2 seconds

When John Z. De Lorean was arrested by FBI agents on charges of drug-trafficking, in October 1982, his dream of a world-beating sportscar seemed finally over. In 1984 De Lorean was cleared of the drug charges and since then he has often spoken of starting again to build his 'ethical car'. So far, however, all that remains of his dream is a vast number of unanswered legal and financial questions and a small number of De Lorean DMC-12 sportscars.

Both the commercial story and the car itself were more the stuff of Hollywood than of Detroit; and both will be remembered as failures. Unfortunately so, because if De Lorean's methods were suspect, his aim, to build a new generation of safety-conscious sportscar, was worthy.

The bare bones of the convoluted commercial story are that De Lorean was a respected, if flamboyant, former General Motors top executive. Having outlined his plans, he eventually persuaded the British government to back his venture to the tune of several hundred million dollars, to manufacture his technically advanced car in depressed Northern Ireland. He set up his factory near Belfast and, with a lot of help from Lotus and Colin Chapman, adapted his fairly unworkable original designs to produce a more viable car. Viable, that is, in engineering terms, because early in 1982, after endless delays and scandals, the company collapsed and the questions began. De Lorean had built a little over 5,000 cars in all, of which about 4,000 went to the USA. Ironically, some sold at well over cost after the company's collapse, where only months earlier they could hardly be sold at all.

They were exciting cars, and but for all the problems might have developed into something good, but any appreciation of the car as it exists is not much more than a look at a final prototype.

De Lorean's original intentions, dating from the mid-1970s, were to build a rear-engined, Ford V6-powered, two-seater coupé, with many high-tech features. A light composite material was to be used for the chassis, clad in a body of unpainted stainless steel, styled by Giugiaro, and based on the Tapiro, an exercise he completed for Porsche in 1970. Its gull-wing doors were one seeming contradiction to its safety conscious intentions.

In the end, a new body moulding process, with

different materials, was developed by Lotus, who also made the rear-engined design workable by giving the De Lorean a backbone chassis. The stainless steel cladding and gull-wing doors were retained and pilot production started in mid-1980.

The car now featured the all-alloy 2.8-litre Peugeot-Renault-Volvo V6 engine, which, with fuel injection delivered 156bhp and 173lb ft of torque, through a five-speed gearbox. The production suspension used coil springs and unequal length arms at the front, with semi-trailing arms and upper and lower links at the rear. The brakes were ventilated discs all round and the car was a lot heavier than it was supposed to be, largely due to De Lorean's insistence on trimming it to Detroit limousine standards, with leather upholstery, power everything, a built-in stereo system and even air conditioning as standard.

Nevertheless, the DMC-12 went well enough in a straight line, partly because of a fairly respectable drag coefficient. The few European examples (including a handful of right-hand-drive cars) would do 135mph/216kph and 0-60 in a little over eight seconds, but strangled US models with maybe 30bhp less could hardly get out of their own way, 110mph/176kph wasn't enough for a supposed sportscar, even if it was twice the national speed limit.

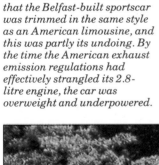

LEFT *John De Lorean insisted that the Belfast-built sportscar was trimmed in the same style as an American limousine, and this was partly its undoing. By the time the American exhaust emission regulations had effectively strangled its 2.8-litre engine, the car was overweight and underpowered.*

Thanks to Lotus, the handling was better than it had any right to be, but not as good as a real sportscar should be. Larger rear tyres subdued the inherent oversteer but the car still hadn't quite made up its mind whether it was a Lambo or a limo.

It was a wasted opportunity; with more attention to the nuts and bolts and a lot less hype it could have been good enough to give Detroit the shake-up that John Z. undoubtedly intended.

BELOW *The everlasting car? The stylish, stainless steel bodyshell of the De Lorean, with its futuristic gullwing doors, provided the basis for the time machine in the film* Back to the Future.

1985 FERRARI TESTAROSSA

The name Testarossa is legendary, and Enzo Ferrari is not a man to treat legends lightly, yet when the successor to the 512 Berlinetta Boxer was revealed, in 1984, the name seemed entirely appropriate.

Literally, it translates as Redhead, a name which doesn't derive from this fastest Ferrari's fiery temperament but from the colour of the red crackle finish of its cam covers. The first Testarossa appeared almost 30 years before the current model, in 1956, as a sports racing prototype. According to some accounts, there was none of the more normally used black crackle heat resistant paint in the works when the first Testarossa engine was being completed and red was the first colour to hand for the cam cover; so the car gained a factory nickname which stuck.

The series of 3-litre V12 sports racing Testarossas which developed from that first prototype were campaigned by Ferrari in international events between 1957 and 1962, with exceptional results even by Ferrari's standards, including, inevitably, the greatest sportscar race of all, Le Mans.

In spite of its staggering performance, the current Testarossa is not (and was never intended to be) a racing car; it is a reasonably civilized road car, which won't ever lull the driver with false luxury, but won't make him suffer undue discomforts for his performance either.

Between the distinctive red cam covers lies a further developed version of Ferrari's 4.9-litre coil springs, telescopic dampers and anti-roll bars all round.

The rack-and-pinion steering is heavy enough to reflect the size of the tyres and of the car itself, but it is also very communicative, feeding back plenty of information and responding with rapid precision. As might be expected, the grip is enormous and for all practical purposes the handling is neutral; to promote either understeer or oversteer other than deliberately would require a fairly hamfisted approach. The brakes are extremely powerful and reliable – just as they should be with such huge ventilated discs – but they do require a delicate touch at low speeds. At the other end of the scale, The Testarossa's Pininfarina styled body shape, drawn up with plenty of reference to the wind tunnel, gives unflappable high-speed stability.

The overall feel of the new generation Testarossa is of a car which has finally come of age. The dynamic shortcomings of the Boxer are no more; refinement has taken this particular Redhead to quite new heights.

ABOVE AND OVERLEAF *Redheads rule! The latest version of the Ferrari Testarossa lives up to the sporting pedigree of its predecessors. The wind-tunnel-developed body makes the car extraordinarily stable at high speed.*

1986 FERRARI TESTAROSSA	
Engine	Flat 12-cyl, 4ohc, 48v
Capacity	4.9 litres
Maximum power	390bhp
Chassis/suspension	Mid-engine multi-tubular spaceframe, coil spring iars
Top speed	180mph
0–60mph	4.9 seconds

1985 MG EX-E

Since the mid-1960s and the steady growth of restrictive. supposedly safety-oriented legislation, the traditional sportscar has been pushed further and further into the background; but, contrary to many opinions, it hasn't disappeared yet. It may be restricted by relatively low production levels and consequently high manufacturing costs to either the smaller specialists or the true giants, but it is still with us; even though the hot hatchback and the sporty coupé have become the surrogate sportscars of the 1980s, there is still, conspicuously, a future for the real thing. It may never be quite so simple, cheap or cheerful as in the golden days between the wars and through the 1950s, but so long as there are enthusiastic drivers,there will always be cars which fit our broad definition of the sportscar.

Somehow, it seems particularly appropriate to look at the sportscar's future through a car shown off by one of the greatest names of the past: MG.

MG, creators of the T-series, the Midget, the MGB and several entire generations of sportscar enthusiasts, had at one time seemed consigned to a future as no more than an evocative model badge on 'sporty' saloons within the British Austin-Rover range; but at the Frankfurt Motor Show late in 1985 they showed, in sensational style, that neither they nor the sportscar were finished yet.

The prototype that they showed was dubbed the MG EX-E and it created as much of a stir in 1985 as many predecessors have in the past.

The sleek, high-tech body is made of a self-coloured, injection-moulded plastic and covers a stiff, bonded-aluminium spaceframe. It is strictly a two-seater and has superb low-drag aerodynamics. The mid-mounted engine and five-speed transmission of the prototype are derived from the Austin-Rover Group's successful four-wheel-drive Metro 6R4 rally car and like that car the EX-E offers permanent all-wheel drive, with a sophisticated viscous coupling system and limited slip differentials front and rear.

The EX-E has variable rate power steering, an anti-lock system for its four-wheel ventilated disc brakes (common now on high performance saloons, but a rarity on sportscars), variable, cockpit adjustable ride-height for optimum aerodynamic performance, and even electronic proximity warning devices for low speed manoeuvering. Most of its high-

RIGHT AND ABOVE RIGHT
Although only a concept development car, Austin-Rover Group's MG EX-E gives a taste of the sort of sportscars we are likely to be driving in the future. Ultra-low, sleek bodystyles, with computer-

controlled everything is the norm. Instrumentation as we know it is replaced by head-up displays projected on to the windscreen – a development currently being used on fighter aircraft.

198? MG EX-E	
Engine	V6, 4ohc, 24v
Capacity	3.0 litres
Maximum power	250bhp
Chassis/suspension	Mid-engine, bonded aluminium spaceframe, four-wheel drive
Top speed	—
0–60mph	—

technology dynamic features are microchip-based and there are further looks into the future in card-key entry and service systems, road condition monitoring and in-dash navigation aids. Its sumptuously finished cockpit also features sophisticated but workable electronic instrumentation and controls which mark the EX-E as a real car of the future and not just a show special.

Although the rally Metro's all-alloy, 3-litre, four-valve-per-cylinder V6 engine is detuned in the EX-E from over 400bhp to a more docile 250bhp or so, it still offers enough power to promise supercar levels of performance without temperament. Part of its appeal for the rally car was that a big, normally aspirated engine would be both more responsive and more reliable than a smaller, more highly stressed turbo engine – and those are just as important in the MG application.

So far, the futuristic MG is just that, a possibility for the future, but there is little reason to doubt projected performance figures of approaching 170mph/272kph and 0-60mph/96kph in only five seconds and the car's chassis specification, on paper at least, seems more than good enough to handle all this urge. What's more, its stunning good looks speak for themselves, and that more than anything else may prompt the car's originators to take the next vital step, into building running prototypes.

Whether or not the EX-E ever becomes a production reality, it has served its purpose as a pointer to what is possible for the sportscar in a technological age where enthusiasm still lives.

The face of things to come.
The sportscar is dead.
Long live the sportscar!

1985 PONTIAC FIERO

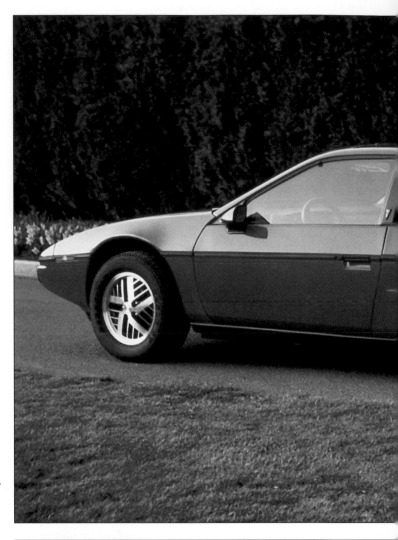

Apart from the evergreen Corvette and a few low volume specials and replicas, America hasn't had much to offer by way of sportscars since the mid-1960s. Perhaps the change of public attitudes that followed Ralph Nader's scathing attack on the Chevy Corvair in *Unsafe at Any Speed* gave the big US manufacturers the final excuse. Privately, they may have been glad of a reason to shun the sportscar business even more totally than they had in the past. In pure sales terms it would hurt them very little to leave the low volume specialist market to the Europeans (who always had them beaten anyway), and latterly to the Japanese.

And even if you had expected a sportscar for the 1980s from the USA, it is highly unlikely that you would have dreamed of it being mid-engined, plastic-bodied – and coming from Pontiac.

Yet with the Fiero, introduced in 1983, the least likely GM division produced a car that was at once stylish, innovative, admirably functional and – in its chassis at least – quite capable of taking on many of Europe's and Japan's best.

It was based on a steel inner shell, with a prominent backbone, on which all the mechanical bits append to make a completely driveable rolling chassis. This is then clothed in an all-plastic outer shell, attached to machined locating pads to ensure perfect panel fit.

It was clever, pretty and, as launched, a frustrating disappointment to real enthusiasts, because Pontiac had failed to go the whole way. They had launched the mid-engined coupé as a sporty commuter car rather than a sportscar, with an old and asthmatic 91bhp, 2.5-litre, four-cylinder, cast-iron engine that left it barely able to get out of its own way. With this engine, the dynamic abilities of the Fiero were wasted. It struggled to achieve 100mph or to reach 60mph in much less than 12 seconds even in manual gearbox form, and such figures hardly matched the appeal of the sporty two-seater's looks.

The cure came within a year, as Pontiac gave the Fiero a rather more exciting fuel-injected 2.8-litre V6. It was just as suitable for the mid-engine location but, in the GT version (which also has slightly stiffer springing than the base model, minor styling changes and an optional rear wing), it offered almost 50 per cent more power, up to 140bhp at 5,200rpm,

1986 PONTIAC FIERO GT	
Engine	V6, ohv
Capacity	2.8 litres
Maximum power	140bhp
Chassis/suspension	Mid-engine, backbone/inner shell, coil spring ifs, Chapman strut irs
Top speed	127mph
0–60mph	8.0 seconds

ABOVE AND LEFT *American dream – or nightmare? In the Pontiac Fiero, General Motors at last have a car to take on the sportscars of Europe and Japan. Mid-engined and plastic-bodied, with superb handling, the Fiero embodies all the latest in sportscar technology, but throws it all away with its outdated under-powered engine.*

and an equally useful 170lb ft of torque.

The Fiero was still no lightweight, at well over a ton, but at least it could now deliver the sort of performance its looks promised. In GT form its top speed went up to over 125mph/200kph and the 0-60 time came down to a far more respectable 8 seconds – both figures comfortably better than US versions of the very similar looking and only slightly cheaper Toyota MR2, which is generally accepted as the standard setter in the small sportscar class.

The Fiero GT, which sits on wider alloy wheels and low profile tyres, can also give the MR2 a run for its money in terms of handling, roadholding and ride, which is no mean achievement.

Suspension is by unequal length wishbones at the front and a Chapman strut arrangement with lower wishbones at the rear, with coil springs, telescopic dampers and anti-roll bars at both ends. Being a heavy car with shortish suspension travel, the Fiero's ride is necessarily firm and the rear weight bias is noticeable near its limits, especially on lifting suddenly from the throttle.

The steering, while feeling sharp enough, is slower than the sportscar norm but there is enough built-in understeer to make the Fiero inherently very safe for all but the clumsiest driver. Its all-round disc brakes are also very competent except for a tendency to fade a little after repeated hard use – another reflection of the car's weight.

Again like the MR2, one big area where the Fiero succeeds in bringing small sportscars into the 1980s is in comfort and build quality. It has an excellent driving position (with a tilting steering wheel option for anyone who still thinks entry is difficult in spite of the large doors) and very good visibility except for the inevitable three-quarter rear problem.

1985 TOYOTA MR2

Until 1985, only the Fiat empire had been brave enough to offer the mid-engined format on a mass-produced small sportscar. They had done it twice; once successfully, with the pioneering and highly regarded X1/9, and once disastrously, with the slightly larger Lancia Beta Monte Carlo: not a bad car but a failure.

There was no doubting the theoretical advantages of the mid-engined layout, at least not when it was properly sorted out, and it had few drawbacks other than making luggage space a problem – which was not the biggest consideration with two seats.

The layout had already become virtually indispensible at the grown-up end of the supercar market, and if for no better reason than emulating big-brother you might have expected *somebody* to build another mid-engined small car. Strangely though, what little was left of the mass-produced sportscar industry in the mid-1980s (when the hot hatchback had become the almost universal sportscar surrogate), remained almost laughably conservative. What little creative instinct remained seemed more directed at creating replicas of what had gone than designs for what might be.

Nevertheless, if you had had to say where a new mid-engined sportscar might come from, you would more likely have named one of those small European specialists than a Japanese giant.

And then the car which re-wrote the script for all other small sportscar builders in the mid-1980s came from the biggest of them all, Toyota: steady, uninspiring Toyota who hadn't even looked at the sportscar market for 20 years.

Toyota's MR2 was a winner from the moment it was revealed in 1985. It is what the Lancia might have been, a bigger S1/9 with more power, more room and more refinement. In typically Japanese style, it invented nothing new but perfected much that already exists.

The 1.6-litre twin-cam four-cylinder engine is mounted transversely between the cockpit and rear axle line, driving through a sweet, close-ratio five-speed gearbox, which, for once, isn't ruined by a linkage to the rear.

This 16-valve, injected engine is a free-revving gem (derived from the front-wheel-drive Corolla hatchback). It peaks with 122bhp at 6,600rpm, with exceptional smoothness and throttle response throughout the rev range. The straightline performance is comfortably ahead of the old X1/9, at 122mph/195.2kph and 0-60mph/96kph in only eight seconds, but the MR2's real excellence is in its roadholding, handling, brakes and overall dynamic feel.

Judged on those criteria, it is in a class of its own in this price sector and has caused the few remaining makers of 'conventional' mass-produced sportscars all manner of headaches.

On MacPherson strut suspension, it has all the flair, instant response and outstanding roadholding

BELOW *There is nothing new under the sun, and it is the Japanese car giant Toyota that has bought the mass-produced mid-engined sports coupé to the world's attention again with their MR2.*

1986 TOYOTA MR2	
Engine	In-line, 4-cyl, 2ohc, 16v
Capacity	1.6 litres
Maximum power	122bhp
Chassis/suspension	Mid-engine, unitary construction, MacPherson strut iars
Top speed	122mph
0–60mph	8.0 seconds

BELOW AND OVERLEAF *The power plant for the MR2 is a 1.6 litre twin-cam unit, mounted transversely just behind the cockpit. The mid-engine layout gives the car near-faultless handling and ride.*

of many true supercars – more, in fact, than most, plus the near-faultless ride comfort of a far bigger car.

It has most of the comfort and equipment levels of a much bigger and more expensive car too; not for the Japanese that notion that sportscar drivers will settle for second best when it comes to accommodation. Unlike the X1/9, the MR2 is only available as a hardtop – albeit with a large, removable glass sunroof.

It is roomy, comfortable, with all the clear instrumentation and well-thought-out controls of a proper sportscar, plus such refinements as in-car-entertainment, electric windows, central locking and other features more typical of an up-market hatchback.

It looks marvellous, stops on the proverbial sixpence, and it even has an acceptable amount of luggage space. More than any car since the original X1/9, it has redefined the rules for small sportscar excellence – and at a time when the very idea of the sportscar was in danger of disappearing. Surely this time the competitors can't simply sit back and ignore the challenge.

The Toyota MR2 has quite a chunky outline for a sports car, and its 0–60mph/0–96kph is not impressive, but for comfort and price it is hard to beat.

1986 ASTON MARTIN ZAGATO

For a company that has been so many times to the brink of extinction, Aston Martin lacks nothing in public self confidence. In 1960, during one of its brief spells of relative stability (this one following the considerable achievement of winning both Le Mans and the World Sports Car Manufacturers' Championship in 1959), Aston introduced its greatest road-legal, semi-competition car, the lovely DB4GT Zagato.

Its voluptuous, lightweight body, built over a light, strong, tubular frame, housed a 314bhp version of Aston's 3.7-litre twin-cam straight-six engine. It gave the short-wheelbase car 150mph/241kph-plus performance, but it was not an easy car to drive and most were used only for racing, where they were overshadowed by the Ferrari 250GTO, which was no great disgrace.

In 1985, Aston, healthy again and brimming over with enthusiasm, announced a new association with Zagato. Their planned new model would be the company's fastest road car ever; in fact, with an uprated version of the Vantage engine in a smaller, lighter car, it would be one of the fastest cars in the world.

At the outset, the only tangible evidence of Aston's intentions was several artists' impressions and a welter of words in the press – including projected numbers such as 187mph/301kph and sub-five-second 0-60 times. These would make the second generation Aston Martin Zagato not just *one* of the fastest production cars in the world, but *the* fastest – quicker even than Ferrari's latest Testarossa or GTO, or the Lamborghini Countach QV.

Yet it would be a conventional, front-engined car, frankly described as an adapted Vantage. Even in the

wake of the mid-engined Nimrod sports racing cars, Aston Martin was not prepared to take the plunge for the road.

More cynical observers took the 'believe-it-when-you-see-it' stance, while Aston Martin started taking substantial deposits on the strictly limited production run of 50 cars – all on the strength of little more than a promise.

By August 1985, however, every car was spoken for and, incredibly, in April 1986 Aston Martin showed not one interim dummy, but three fully-trimmed running production cars at and outside the Geneva Show. They were built and trimmed by Zagato in Italy, with alloy and re-inforced polyester bodies on rolling chassis shipped from Britain.

The original 1960s Zagato was a hard act to follow in terms of outstanding looks, but the 1986 Vantage Zagato stole the show. Built on a much modified Vantage floorplan, the Vantage Zagato was strictly a two-seater coupé, with a traditional Aston Martin grille shape cleverly incorporated into the smooth, moulded nose, between four, big, rectangular headlights. Only a hefty bonnet (hood) bulge (imposed by retaining carburettors on the Vantage engine) intruded into otherwise notably smooth lines. This did not spoil an impressive drag coefficient.

Suddenly, the Vantage Zagato in the flesh opened disturbing possibilities for the cynics that Aston's big-number claims might be more than hype. For one thing, the car was significantly smaller than the Vantage (no slouch itself) and it had a far better drag coefficient. Its claimed 425bhp from the modified engine (with higher compression, improved breathing and more extreme camshafts) was a good 50bhp more than the Vantage but perfectly credible. According to Aston, this engine in a Vantage shell, stripped to match the Zagato's weight, if not its aerodynamic excellence, had already managed 175mph/281.5kph and 0-60mph/96.5kph in 4.7 seconds – the latter in first gear!

As with any supercar in this stratospheric performance league, few owners are likely to come any closer to the genuine top speed than reading properly calibrated test track figures in the 'legitimate' motoring press.

Whether or not the Zagato can match its claims, it is unlikely that any of the 50 examples will follow in the original Zagato's wheeltracks as a full-time racer. It is far more likely that they could eventually match the old car's status as a highly prized classic, and perhaps even compete with Jaguar in the American market.

1986 ASTON MARTIN VANTAGE ZAGATO	
Engine	V8, 4ohc
Capacity	5.4 litres
Maximum power	432bhp
Chassis/suspension	Platform chassis, coil spring/wishbone ifs, De Dion rear, Watts
Top speed	187mph
0–60mph	4.7 seconds

LEFT *This high-performance version of the Vantage engine allows a top speed of 187mph.*

FAR LEFT AND BELOW *Probably the ultimate in exclusivity the 1986 Zagato is Aston Martin's most powerful, fastest and most stylish model to date.*

1986 CHEVROLET CORVETTE

To American car enthusiasts, the Corvette long ago ceased to be just another sports car and became more of an institution. It is no longer just any American sports car, it is *the* American sports car, the one that any fan will defend to the death against puny European hardware, the one that can beat Porsches in the Sports Car Club of America stock racing classes and one of the few American sports cars which has built up any kind of European following, in a market where the traffic across the Atlantic is almost entirely in the opposite direction.

The Corvette survives because it has kept its integrity while moving with the times and although the nameplate has had its ups and downs it has always managed to come back – to the extent that its long-term future will probably be as a separate marque within the General Motors empire.

Since the 1953 shaky start of the underpowered little roadster with the wheezy six-cylinder engine

and the hopeless automatic transmission, there have only really been four distinct restyles. The last of them, in 1982, brought the shape right up to date with the clean, uncluttered lines which survive on to the 1986 car.

It was the introduction of V8 power and a manual gearbox in 1956 which really got the Corvette off the mark as a serious sports car, and since then it has had a formidable list of big and small block V8 options. The weakest was the mid-1970s small block which could only muster a rather feeble 165 bhp, but at the other end of the scale, in 1970, at the height of the musclecar age, there was the 460 bhp 7.4-litre big block. The same year also saw the most potent of the smaller engines, with a very impressive 370 bhp. The same 350 cu. in./875 c.c. capacity survives in today's small block model and with multi-point fuel injection it gives a very useful 240 bhp – a sure sign that performance is making something of a comeback in

the US markets of the mid-1980s.

Better still, the latest Corvette is a car which can make full use of that power, with chassis performance which will give a lot of supposedly superior European cars a fair run for their money. Its glassfibre and reinforced-plastic body sits on a steel chassis whose all-round independent suspension uses transverse glassfibre leaf springs front and rear. Until recently the car was almost universally condemned for having a ride that was too firm for its own good, but it was softened up quite markedly for 1986, to the point where it is now firm but forgiving. The overall effect is helped by superb seats and interior appointments including electronic instrumentation with a mixture of analog and digital readouts.

Chassis refinement runs to a limited slip differential as standard, a four-speed manual gearbox with overdrive on no less than three of the ratios, and ABS anti-lock brakes. There are only 2½ turns of the wheel from lock to lock, with perhaps a shade too much power assistance for some tastes, though the steering is very precise.

On the road, the lazy, torquey engine gives pretty rapid progress by any standards, with 0–60 mph/0 96 kph times down below six seconds and a top speed in the order of 150 mph/240 kph – given enough road. The motor revs slowly by European standards but it has both excellent response and a lovely growl,

and of course, with all that stump-pulling, low down torque it has incredible flexibility.

The handling tends heavily towards understeer, easily neutralized by lifting off the power and with power oversteer fairly easily on-tap – but it is not a car whose limits should be explored by the unwary, all that weight takes a little catching once it does let go.

More than ever perhaps, the Corvette is a true sports car which can mix it with the best of them, and there is little reason to believe that it won't still be carrying the banner for a long time to come.

1986 CHEVROLET CORVETTE	
Engine	V8, ohv
Capacity	5.7 litres
Maximum power	240bhp
Chassis/suspension	Steel chassis, GRP body, tl/wishbone ifs, tl/multiple link irs
Top speed	151mph
0–60mph	6.5 seconds

BELOW *The Chevrolet Corvette is a mighty entrant in the sports car stakes, with stylish handling and a quick* 0–60mph/0–96kph *start. It is a formidable rival to the European competition.* INSET *The small-block, powerful V8 engine.*

1986 MAZDA RX-7

Drive a Mazda RX-7, and the uncanny smoothness of its engine confirms something out of the ordinary about this attractive Japanese coupé. In fact, the RX-7 is not just out of the ordinary, it is unique among sportscars in its choice of engine.

Where every other sportscar in the word uses the traditional reciprocating piston engine, the Mazda uses the brilliantly simple Wankel rotary engine, an engine that offers wide-ranging benefits but enough technical problems to have restricted it to a handful of production applications.

Dr Felix Wankel's engine, which basically comprises a three-sided rotor following a four-stroke cycle within an outer casing, was developed during the 1950s by Wankel and the German car and motorcycle maker NSU. The engine solved the problem of converting the energy of burning fuel directly into rotary motion, but there were serious practical problems with sealing the rotor tips and with excessive fuel consumption.

NSU never really did solve the problems themselves, although they did make several Wankel-engined cars, the first of them a sports version of the NSU Sport Prinz, introduced in 1963.

By this time, Mazda too were committed to building rotary-engined cars, having entered a licensing agreement with NSU in 1961. The first Mazda rotary was shown in 1963, just weeks after NSU's first, but like the NSU it still had problems. Part of Mazda's solution was to try multi-rotor engines, and they eventually settled on the twin-rotor format used in today's RX-7. Their first rotary-engined production car, the 110S coupé, went on sale in 1967. Mazda has continued rotary engine development ever since, alone after NSU abandoned the format in 1977.

ABOVE *Mazda's latest RX-7 coupé is powered by the turbine-smooth, Wankel rotary engine. Only Mazda have persevered with the rotary, and it has finally paid off with a powerful smooth-running, twin-rotor unit that endows it with performance akin to that of a Porsche 924S. Even more* remarkable is that the rotary engine does this with an engine of just over 1.3 litres, yet delivers performance similar to a 2.4-litre engine. To get round this apparent disparity, the capacity of the rotary engine has to be multiplied by 1.8 to give an equivalent cylinder capacity.

1986 MAZDA RX-7	
Engine	Twin-rotor Wankel rotary
Capacity	2.6 litres
Maximum power	148bhp
Chassis/suspension	Unitary construction, MacPherson strut ifs, multi-link irs
Top speed	133mph
0–60mph	8.5 seconds

By the end of 1978, Mazda had built over one million rotary-engined cars and launched the first RX-7; since then, the RX-7 has achieved exceptional sales success in both Europe and America and overcome all the Wankel's inherent problems save its excessive thirst. Between 1978 and 1985, Mazda sold almost half a million RX-7s, comfortably outselling its most obvious rival, the Porsche 924. Late in 1985 they launched the second generation RX-7, aimed this time at Porsche 944 territory; it had new body styling, a clever new suspension system and a 2.6-litre version of the trusty twin-rotor engine – giving 148bhp at 6,500rpm and 135lb/ft of torque at only 3,000rpm for superb flexibility and smoothness.

Like its predecessor, the latest RX-7 is very well equipped for a sportscar, with such standard fittings as an electric sunroof, electric windows, an up-market stereo system, air-conditioning for the US market and much more; yet it still behaves like a true sportscar. Top speed is almost 135mph in European spec, or almost 130mph even for the USA, with 0-60mph times in the region of 8 seconds, with sparkling mid-range performance. In deference to keeping the free-revving engine in one piece, a buzzer indicates its 7,000rpm limit, well before tip-seal damage is likely to occur.

The new suspension is excellent. The front uses MacPherson struts with lower A-arms, coil springs and an anti-roll bar, but the real novelty is at the back, which is a multi-link system with floating hubs, coil springs and an anti-roll bar – with telescopic dampers all-round.

The main feature of the 'Dynamic Tracking' rear suspension is variable geometry, which allows a small degree of initial toe-out during cornering (for very precise turn-in) changing to a degree of toe-in, which helps neutralize oversteer. It is even more complicated than it sounds, but it works. Coupled with adjustable damping rates and superb variable rate power steering, it gives the RX-7 very high levels of grip (especially in the wet), very precise responses and even a reasonably good ride.

In sticking with the rotary-engined concept, Mazda have evolved not only a unique sportscar, but also a thoroughly competent one, which went one stage further early in 1986 with the introduction of an even more potent turbo version. The only problem which still remains is heavy fuel consumption, but that never seems to have bothered sportscar buyers unduly.

1986 Reliant Scimitar SS1 Ti

When the small English car-maker Reliant introduced their distinctive little plastic-bodied Scimitar SS1 two-seater early in 1985, they were reviving a breed of car which most people thought had died with the last MG Midgets and Triumph Spitfires many years before. They were bringing back the affordable small sports car, not quite mass-produced in the big corporate sense, but a legitimate production model and much more than the usual run of the kit-car market.

Reliant was the perfect company to launch such a car. It had long experience of building relatively short-run models with glassfibre bodies and 'bought-in' running gear. Reliant even has a worldwide reputation for designing cars and setting up entire manufacturing plants for countries such as Israel,

An Italian-styled British sports car, the Reliant Scimitar has proved popular in the United States. Princess Anne probably gave sales a boost when she was caught speeding in her Scimitar!

India and assorted Mediterranean and Caribbean countries which need rugged, straightforward cars in relatively small numbers. Reliant's bread-and-butter models, using their own excellent lightweight engines, are three-wheel saloons and small vans taking advantage of British tax concessions, plus limited numbers of four-wheel derivatives.

For many years, Reliant also built the larger, glassfibre-bodied, Ford-engined Scimitar sports car, which started life as a coupé and grew into the unique Scimitar sporting estate, to which a drophead model was eventually added. For better or worse the new Scimitar spelled the end of development for the previous model but took nothing from the old car except its name. It was based on an engine size midway between Reliant's own four-cylinder and the 2.8-litre Ford V6 of the big Scimitar, and launched with a choice of two engines, a rather flaccid 69 bhp 1.3-litre four-cylinder Ford engine, or the 96 bhp, 1.6-litre Ford four-cylinder from the Escort XR3.

Its fabricated steel chassis with independent suspension all round, by wishbones and coil springs at the front and semi-trailing arms and coil springs at the rear, was excellent, but the looks of its Michelotti-designed body, with integral bumpers and pop-up headlights, were widely criticized. Virtually every reviewer thought the car could handle more power.

At least the bolted-on glassfibre panels made the SS1 very distinctive and kept insurance costs low, and it did have the biggest of all advantages for a sports car – it was a full convertible.

In mid-1986, Reliant solved the power problem by offering the Scimitar in Ti form, with a 135 bhp version of the Nissan Silvia 1.8-litre four-cylinder turbo engine, plus the five-speed gearbox that went with it. This excellent engine fitted into the SS1 with virtually no other changes but it completely transformed the car's performance and made it a sports car worthy of the name. The 0–60 mph/0–96 kph acceleration time came down from over 11 seconds for the 1.6-litre car to barely 7 seconds – quick by most standards. Top speed went up from not much better than 105 mph/168 kph to comfortably over 125 mph/ 200 kph. It was a stunning transformation.

Yet the chassis handles it with great character. There is a tendency towards wheelspin and power oversteer but the car is so predictable and easy to drive that every ounce of performance can be exploited by even reasonably competent drivers. It gives the mid-engined Toyota MR2, the car which re-defined the mid-1980s sports car market, a good run for its money and is markedly cheaper – if admittedly less refined. With a mixture of disc and drum brakes in a very lightweight package it stops exceptionally well and everything about it, from its compact size to its exceptionally responsive engine,

1986 RELIANT SCIMITAR SS1 Ti	
Engine	Nissan, 4-cyl, in-line, turbo
Capacity	1.8 litres
Maximum power	135bhp
Chassis/suspension	Fabricated steel, GRP body, coil spring/wishbone ifs, trailing arm irs
Top speed	125mph
0–60mph	7.0 seconds

make it a very rapid car from point to point on everyday roads. And, of course, when the sun shines the top comes off, which is still one of the real tests of a true sports car.

Perhaps the critics are right and the SS1 should have been styled by the new wave of English stylists, rather than in Italy, but as a drivers' car it is a worthy successor to the sports cars of old.

1986 RENAULT ALPINE GTA V6 TURBO

Renault might not be the most obvious name for a sports car builder but the giant French car company, with its reputation for competent hatchbacks and attractive but not particularly inspiring saloons, nowadays has a turbocharged rear-engined flagship which can give almost any medium-range sports car a run for its money.

The Renault Alpine GTA V6 Turbo is designed by Renault's own engineers and built around Renault running gear in the small and specialized Alpine workshops at Dieppe. Alpine has had a long association with Renault which started in the mid-1950s, when Alpine's founder, former racing driver Jean Redélé, built the first Alpine, a rallying coupé, around Renault 750 parts.

Over the years, the Alpine name became associated with most of Renault's racing and rallying efforts, and in 1970 they became officially responsible for the whole of Renault's competition programme, the greatest achievement in sports racing terms being the team's dominant win in the 1978 Le Mans 24-hour race. The Alpine name was also used on several Renault road cars, as the Renault performance badge yet until the mid-1980s, the Alpine marque was far better known for racing than for its road cars.

It was only with the introduction of the V6-engined Renault-Alpine early in 1984 that Renault began to think of selling a real sports car worldwide. By mid 1986, the car was available in both left- and right-hand drive, for most world markets. Top of the range was the very rapid V6 Turbo.

Unusually for a current sports car, but like the Porsche 911 which is one of its most obvious direct rivals, the GTA is rear-engined. The engine is positioned behind the rear axle-line of the neat backbone chassis. The glassfibre-reinforced monocoque body shell is a reasonably spacious 2+2 seater which even offers a fair amount of baggage space for two people and very good standards of interior trim and equipment. Yet its sleek lines make it one of the most aerodynamic of all production cars – although the wide wheels of the Turbo version do detract a little from the normally-aspirated car's extraordinary efficiency.

The most potent engine is the 2.5-litre V6 with a single overhead camshaft on each cylinder bank and a Garrett turbocharger. This smooth, free-revving unit gives a very healthy 200 bhp with a big spread of torque; coupled to a five-speed gearbox with perfectly chosen ratios it gives the GTA quite exceptional performance, with a top speed of over 150 mph/240 kph and 0–60 mph/0–96 kph acceleration times of less than 6½ seconds.

In general, the Renault is a very capable car and much more practical for everyday use than most exotics, one of its few obvious running faults being that the front baggage compartment has to be opened to gain access to the fuel filler cap.

Its handling is generally, but not always, taut and predictable, with coil springs and double wishbone suspension all round and very precise rack-and-pinion steering, which manages without power assistance thanks to the fairly light front end weight. On the wide tyres of the turbo version, there is a very high level of cornering grip and the suspension, unusually for a French car of any kind, is stiff enough to keep body roll well under control.

What the GTA does lack to some extent is straight line stability at very high speeds in windy conditions, and although the car is always safe, it demands some concentration to drive it in a hurry. There is also a definite degree of turbo lag, which tends to make for exciting progress when driving quickly on twisty, damp roads. Furthermore, the weight of the engine behind the rear axle is always noticeable around the car's very high limits – in much the same way as a Porsche 911.

The Alpine is something very special, having brought a major manufacturer firmly into the exotic sports car market. It is a spectacular car to look at, and is even more spectacular to drive.

RIGHT *The Turbo version of the Alpine, Renault's venture into sports cars, using the Alpine name it has made famous in motor racing. The Alpine GTA is a great car, proving that even the mass production manufacturers can produce classic sports cars if they try.*

1986 RENAULT GTA V6 TURBO	
Engine	V6, turbo
Capacity	2.5 litres
Maximum power	200bhp
Chassis/suspension	Steel backbone, GRP body, coil spring/wishbone all round
Top speed	152mph
0–60mph	6.5 seconds

1986 TVR 390iSE

In a market where smaller specialist sportscar makers have come and gone with frightening regularity, only three or four have survived with any sort of distinction. Morgan and Panther have continued to make a reasonable business out of selling nostalgia, either real or contrived, and TVR has soldiered on with cars of no great pioneering spirit but a legacy of steady, solid development and real character.

The TVR company itself was started in the late 1950s by an enthusiastic special-builder, Trevor Wilkinson, from whose Christian name it took its title. Since then, the small but hugely enthusiastic maker from the famous English seaside funfair town of Blackpool has been through numerous changes of ownership, each of them in turn shrugging off its own financial crises with varying degrees of success.

Concurrent with the frequent commercial changes, the TVR car has developed from Wilkinson's early Ford and Coventry-Climax-engined Granturas, with more and more power, constantly revised and refined chassis and running gear, and just a few fundamental changes of body style. The cars have always just about kept pace with the rest of the world, without ever really changing from Wilkinson's original concept.

Today, TVR is probably stronger than it has ever been, partly due to a long period of stable and efficient management but even more to the continuing success of the angular body style cars which saw the company into the 1980s on the early Tasmin. In coupé and open variants (the latter by far the more popular), the shape has variously used Ford four-cylinder engines, Ford V6 engines of up to 3-litres (though the best of all was the Capri 2.8 injection unit) and, since 1982, the mighty, Buick-based Rover 3.5-litre V8, which, in

RIGHT AND OVERLEAF The stylish simplicity of the TVR 390iSE gives more than a hint of the potential performance from the 3.9-litre, Rover V8-derived engine. A real driver's car, its immense power means the TVR needs more than a little care to prevent the rear end stepping out of line – especially in wet driving conditions.

1986 TVR 390iSE	
Engine	Rover V8, ohv
Capacity	3.9 litres
Maximum power	275bhp
Chassis/suspension	Multi-tubular backbone, coil spring/wishbone iars
Top speed	150mph
0–60mph	5.5 seconds

190bhp fuel-injected form topped the range as the TVR350i until early 1985.

Then TVR went a large step further, by dropping an injected Rover V8, enlarged to 3.9-litres, into their excellent tubular backbone chassis, to create a cut-price supercar chaser – the 390iSE.

Set well back under the beautifully finished fibre-glass shell, this heavily modified all-alloy engine with a claimed 275bhp and 270lb ft of torque turned the TVR convertible from merely quick to stagger-ing. Even hampered by a frustrating lack of traction, the 390iSE would hit 60mph in about 5½ seconds, accompanied by the most glorious noises from the flexible, instant-action V8. And the power went on and on, with 100mph/161kph available in less than 15 seconds and a top speed – given a long enough run – over over 150mph/241kph.

Good as the chassis was, the lusty engine had more than enough power to catch out a lead-footed driver, especially on slow corners and in a low gear – or anytime in the wet if discretion was cast aside. Treated with respect, however, the 390iSE responded with enormous amounts of grip, without allowing any real time for relaxation as the heavy steering fed back steady streams of information in the form of small twitches and suppressed kicks. The ride itself was rock steady, however, with hard springs but ex-cellent damping and body isolation.

In fact, the car was remarkably comfortable for a convertible – or more accurately a semi-Targa-top. The seats are deeply shrouded within the well-trimmed cockpit and the big central tunnel gives unbeatable lateral support – plus the familiar high-sited TVR gearchange.

The TVR roof is an object lesson in simplicity, a rigid central panel which clips easily in and out between the top of the steeply-raked windscreen and the rear, folding hood (top), which flips up and down in one simple action. When it is up it is waterproof and solid; down, it is commendably free from buffet-ing.

The TVR has many similar assets, with just enough slightly rough edges to remind the driver, if he should need reminding, that this is not just another soulless, mass-produced design from the big batallions; it is a car of character.

1987 CADILLAC ALLANTE

In most ways, the Cadillac Allante's inclusion here under the label of 'sports car' is something of a cheat, but in another way it deserves to be included as an illustration of the way the market may be headed in the future in the biggest of all markets, the USA.

The Allante doesn't have particularly sparkling performance by the best European sports car standards, and it isn't particularly high-tech, even though it does use clever electronic analog instruments and anti-lock brakes. It is a sporty two-seater with a soft top and Italian styling, and it typifies a change of direction which many observers see as only the beginning of pastures new for the greatest of American 'quality' car builders. It is what you might call a significant model.

There were several good reasons behind the birth of the Allante, principally the growing prestige of European sporting luxury cars such as Mercedes and Jaguar in the American market in recent years, and their steadily-increasing prices relative to domestic models. There was also a new corporate structure for Cadillac itself, which recently lost its own manufacturing facilities within the General Motors empire, but was compensated by the new freedom to shop around for its major engineering elements. Fortunately, Cadillac has engineering management with the vision to take advantage of such circumstances.

So, enter the Allante, late in 1986. It is an open two-seater, sleekly styled with a high waistline, steeply-raked windscreen and a wide, low look. It has a high-quality convertible top and a detachable aluminium hardtop which should spend the summer months in the garage. It is built on a shortened version of Cadillac's Eldorado platform chassis, with that car's MacPherson strut front suspension with lower arms and trailing links, plus Chapman strut rear suspension with lower wishbones and a transverse glassfibre leaf spring. The chassis goes all the way to Italy for its Pininfarina clothing, mostly in steel but with a few aluminium panels, and then back to Detroit for its running gear.

That too comes largely from the Eldorado, with a fuel-injected version of the alloy-block 4.1-litre V8, upgraded to give 170 bhp — a rather paltry specific output by European standards where a 4-litre engine would be looking for somewhere nearer 250 bhp to be worthy of being called sporty, but not bad when you realise that power has to go through the front wheels only. The engine is mounted transversely and drives through an uprated four-speed automatic transmission — sticking with automatic is another sign that Cadillac hasn't quite gone all the way to thinking of the Allante as a sports car.

On the other hand the Allante has all-round disc brakes with the most sophisticated Bosch ABS anti-locking system as standard, as well as quick ratio rack-and-pinion steering and surprisingly taut suspension — certainly a change from the previous Cadillac norms.

In terms of performance, the Allante, as befits a car weighing almost a ton and a half and with just 170 bhp on tap, only claims a top speed in the region of 120 mph/192 kph and 0–60 mph/0–96 kph in a little under 9½ seconds, which is well behind most European alternatives. The handling and ride are perhaps more European than American, though, helped by specially developed wide, low-profile Goodyear tyres, another area where Cadillac can exert a lot of corporate clout.

It is still difficult to pigeonhole the Allante as a sports car or otherwise, but it is without doubt an interesting pointer to the way American auto makers feel they can go now that 'soft-top' isn't quite such a dirty word as it was at the height of safety lobby power. Cadillac see the Allante as an ultra-luxury specialist car for enthusiastic drivers; many people see it as a glimmer of hope for a new breed of sporty American cars.

RIGHT *The Cadillac Allante is a classic example of the luxury sedan manufacturer's idea of a sports car — an ultra-luxury specialist two-seater with soft top and sporty Italian styling. Yet Cadillac refuses to abandon automatic transmission in favour of the classic sports car stick-shift.*

1987 CADILLAC ALLANTE	
Engine	V8, ohv
Capacity	4.1 litres
Maximum power	170bhp
Chassis/suspension	Platform, Macpherson strut, Chapman strut/wishbone/tl irs
Top speed	120mph
0–60mph	9.3 seconds

INDEX

Page numbers in *italic* refer to illustrations